Exploring *folk* with Wool Appliqué & More

16 Projects Using Embroidery, Rug Hooking & Punch Needle

Rebekah L. Smith *and* Kelsey Anilee Smith

C&T PUBLISHING

Text copyright © 2019 by Rebekah L. Smith and Kelsey Anilee Smith

Photography and artwork copyright © 2019 by C&T Publishing, Inc.

Publisher: Amy Marson

Creative Director: Gailen Runge

Acquisitions Editor: Roxane Cerda

Managing Editor: Liz Aneloski

Editor: Katie Van Amburg

Technical Editor: Julie Waldman

Cover/Book Designer: April Mostek

Production Coordinator: Tim Manibusan

Production Editor: Jennifer Warren

Illustrator: Aliza Shalit

Photo Assistant: Rachel Holmes

Cover photography by Kelly Burgoyne of C&T Publishing, Inc.

Style photography by Laura Webb and instructional photography by Kelly Burgoyne of C&T Publishing, Inc., unless otherwise noted

Published by C&T Publishing, Inc., P.O. Box 1456, Lafayette, CA 94549

Library of Congress Cataloging-in-Publication Data

Names: Smith, Rebekah L. (Rebekah Leigh), 1971- author. | Smith, Kelsey (Kelsey Anilee), author.

Title: Exploring folk art with wool appliqué & more : 16 projects using embroidery, rug hooking & punch needle / Rebekah L. Smith and Kelsey Anilee Smith.

Other titles: Exploring folk art with wool appliqué and more

Description: Lafayette, CA : C&T Publishing, Inc., [2019]

Identifiers: LCCN 2018055630 | ISBN 9781617458132 (soft cover)

Subjects: LCSH: Appliqué--Patterns. | Embroidery. | Rugs, Hooked. | Folk art--United States.

Classification: LCC TT779 .S6219 2019 | DDC 746.44/5--dc23

LC record available at https://lccn.loc.gov/2018055630

Printed in China

10 9 8 7 6 5 4 3 2 1

DEDICATION

To the matriarchs of art in our family, Zella Mohler and Marj "Granny" Smith, who have inspired us with their creativity and love of the textile arts.

ACKNOWLEDGMENTS

This book, more than the previous two (for Rebekah), has been a joint effort, and there are many to whom we are grateful for their help in this endeavor.

We are grateful for the gifts that God has given us; ultimately, all the glory goes to Him in bestowing us with creative abilities that reflect His own.

Our family, as ever, is a steadfast rock in our lives, and at some point everyone plays a role in the process: Bruce as a husband and father who is always there; Karly as a daughter and sister who helps bring our collective creativity out; and Tessa as a daughter and sister who spent many hours bringing our work to the page with her photographs.

This book would not have been possible without the help and talent of some dear friends near and far, who patiently worked with us and made this book become a reality. These women continue to inspire us. Thanks to Donna Bennett, a dear friend and rug-hooker extraordinaire. We thank Cindy Sullivan, a friend whose rug-hooking skills shine. Many thanks to Susan Meyers, the punch-needle queen and our dear friend and talented rug hooker. We thank Lori Ann Corelis, a fellow artist, stitcher, and friend. Thanks to Kathy Wright for many years of friendship, her skills in quilting and yarn sewing, and the use of some of her beautiful antiques as props in our photos. We're always thankful for Christine Miller, mother to Rebekah and grandmother to Kelsey, and a wonderful stitcher.

We could not help getting a few more friends involved, including Debbie Gulland, Patti Wolfe and Ginger Jackson, Patti Gagliardi and Jill Zartler, and Deb Tomschek and Teri Hedrick. Thank you, ladies, for making your own beautiful versions of the projects for the gallery in the back.

We could not do without the talented sewing skills of our friend Rebecca Bihun, and the book would not be as beautiful as it is without Laura Webb, whose time and skill result in pictures that are more lovely than we could imagine.

We extend our thanks to all the folks at C&T for their help in creating this book. Finally, in the spirit of this book, we want to thank all of the creative women in our lives who appreciate our work and work alongside us. You know who you are!

CONTENTS

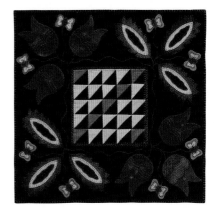
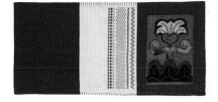

FOREWORD

Being an artist can be lonely. Creativity calls for its fair share of solitude; imagining and artistic decisions happen in a place no one can enter or see.

What can soften the loneliness of the artist? There is, of course, the beauty of the finished work, the smile of delight at the end. The sensation of colors and shapes ordered and worked to point toward something deeper—this is motivating for artists, pushing us through the darkness.

Yet there is nothing quite like having a friend who is an artist, too. Community softens the loneliness whether the friend uses the same materials or not. Sometimes having an artist friend is just what is needed to break through the heavy clouds of a creative block.

As a writer, I am indebted to my writer friends who laugh and ache over words with me. My musician friends teach me the limitations of words. My painter friends teach me about perspective. My carpenter and sculptor friends teach me about structure and depth. My stitcher friends teach me about texture and detail.

My mom, the coauthor of this book, raised my sisters and me to collaborate as artists and share our work. We grew up surrounded by artists, mostly folk artists, who helped my mom see her own work differently and who were always willing to work with her. It comes as no surprise that she and my sister Kelsey would write this book, as Kelsey was my mom's apprentice for some years. The friendships they developed were integral to their growth as artists and their enjoyment of their work. This is why I think my mom was able to translate her painting into wool appliqué and why Kelsey moved so easily from watercolor to embroidery.

As you step into the pages of this book, my hope is that you, too, can develop friendships that take you beyond the limits of your own creativity. The beauty of collaborating is that it makes artists better. You will see your work and your life differently when you make friends with other artists. I encourage you to do at least one of these projects with a friend. You may be surprised at how your art—even your life—changes.

—*Karly A. Smith*

INTRODUCTION

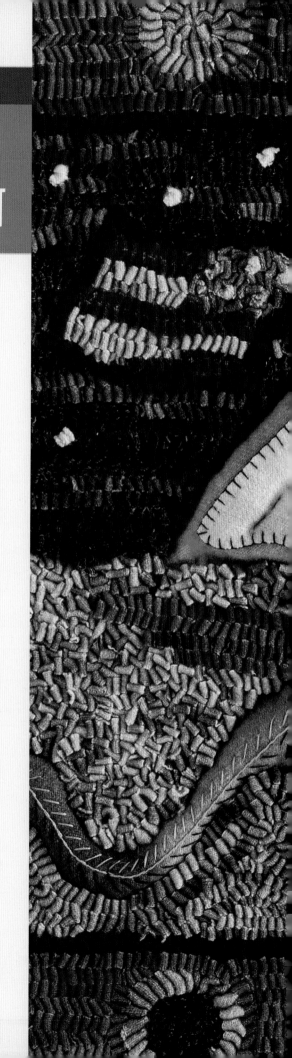

For generations, hand stitching has been a means of building friendships, from the sewing circles of old to the modern-day guild. It has also brought us, a mother-daughter team, even closer.

Many of the techniques used in this book have been inspired by the wool-work our friends do, from rug hooking to punch needle to quilting. Most people we meet on our travels are skilled at more than just appliqué. There are so many ways to use wool, so why stick to one? We wanted to combine techniques to create unique projects for the wool enthusiast.

Knowing we could not do this alone, we gathered up some dear friends to help us make these pieces. Each project has a folk art feel and an extra dose of friendship. In part, we hope to share some lovely friendships (including our own) with you. We also want our fellow stitchers to see how the many kinds of wool arts can be friends, too!

Each project features a collaboration between us or between Rebekah and one of our friends. The projects either have one collaborated work using a combination of techniques or two works that each showcase a different technique.

At the back of the book is a gallery in two parts: the gallery of projects (page 92), where some of our friends have worked our project designs in colorways of their own, and the gallery of friends (page 94), which puts a face to the name for every project collaborator in this book.

We hope our book inspires you to work together with friends and family, as well as to try incorporating new techniques in your woolwork.

—*Rebekah and Kelsey*

Projects

WALLHANGING GARDEN

Techniques:
Wool appliqué
and embroidery

Finished wallhanging: 42″ × 14″

Our first project to share brings embroidery and wool appliqué hand in hand. We just love florals, and the joint design process made this garden tapestry an enjoyable endeavor.

Rebekah designed the wool appliqué squares first, and then I interpreted a square in embroidery. It can be a challenge to go from a medium with an emphasis on blocks of color to a technique that highlights the details. I used a heavily filled embroidery design to echo the look of wool appliqué while still showcasing the textures of wool thread. We wanted the design to coordinate with the appliqué but not copy it. As embroidery does so well, the centerpiece adds some movement to the design with its curved details while maintaining the symmetry.

—*Kelsey*

Photo by Tessa Christine Smith

Sometimes two heads are better than one when it comes to design—especially when they are related!

*This project is a
garden of color for the
walls of your home.*

MATERIALS

Wool appliqué

- 1 antique-white wool rectangle 3″ × 6″ for 6 flower centers

- 1 blue wool square 6″ × 6″ for 4 flowers

- 1 dark-blue wool rectangle 6″ × 8″ for 4 flowers and 2 hearts

- 1 light-green wool square 8″ × 8″ for 4 leafy stems

- 1 green wool square 8″ × 8″ for 4 leafy stems

- 2 tan cotton squares 10″ × 10″ for wool-appliqué diamonds

- Embroidery floss: 1 skein each of antique white (DMC 841), dark brown (DMC 3371), and dark mustard (DMC 829)

- Freezer paper (such as Quilter's Freezer Paper Sheets by C&T Publishing)

Embroidery

- 1 tan cotton square 12″ × 12″ for embroidered diamond

- 1 embroidery stabilizer square 12″ × 12″ for embroidered diamond

- Rustic Wool Moire thread: 1 spool each of dark green (427), medium green (231), turquoise (447), and teal (570)

- Embroidery floss: 1 skein of antique white (DMC 841)

Background

- 1 linen or decorator-cotton rectangle 43″ × 15″ for background

- 1 cotton rectangle 43″ × 15″ for backing

- 1 light-green wool rectangle 3½″ × 15″ for border scallops

- 2 pieces of twill or linen tape, each 6″ long, for hangers

- 1 strip of heavy iron-on interfacing 1″ × 13″ for hanging support

Wool appliqué by Rebekah L. Smith, embroidery by Kelsey Anilee Smith

WOOL APPLIQUÉ

Getting Started

Refer to How to Wool Appliqué (page 77) as needed for additional details on these steps.

1. Cut out the wool appliqué pieces using the pattern (pullout page P1).

2. Lay out the wool project to be sure you have all the pieces.

Making Your Project

Refer to Stitching Your Projects (page 80) for details on the blanket stitch and embroidery stitches.

1. On the first square, stitch the 4 leafy stems into place.

2. Stitch the flowers and the rest of the wool pieces.

3. Repeat Steps 1 and 2 on the second square.

4. Add the embellishment stitches to both squares as desired.

5. Using a steam iron on the wool setting, press the finished pieces on the wrong side.

6. Press a ½″ hem all the way around both finished squares.

Detail of wool appliqué embellishments

EMBROIDERY

Getting Started

Refer to How to Embroider (page 78) as needed for additional details on these steps.

1. Transfer the embroidery pattern (pullout page P1) to the natural linen.

2. Following the manufacturer's directions, iron the embroidery stabilizer to the back of the linen.

Making Your Project

Refer to Stitching Your Projects (page 80) for details on embroidery stitches.

Stitch the pattern using the stitch guide (below). All wool sections are stitched with 2 strands of thread, and all cotton floss sections are stitched with 3 strands.

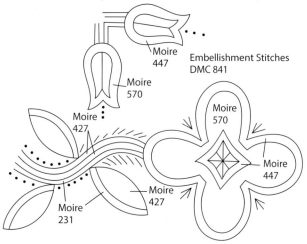

Embroidery stitch guide

1. Stitch the wool sections of the center tulips and stems.

2. To stitch the flowers, outline the flower first using the chain stitch; then outline the diamond in the center.

3. Fill in the rest of the flower with the chain stitch from the outside. Always stitch in a concentric pattern, making your chain stitches go in the same direction.

Detail of the embroidery

4. Once all the flowers are finished, stitch the stems and leaves.

5. Add the cotton embellishment stitches as desired.

6. Using a steam iron on the wool setting, press the finished piece on the wrong side. Place a towel underneath the piece to keep from crushing the embroidery.

7. Trim and press to make a ½″ hem all the way around the cotton square.

FINISHING

1. Press a ½" hem all the way around the outside of the cotton/linen background and the cotton backing fabric.

2. Pin the 3 finished diamonds into place on the background cotton/linen.

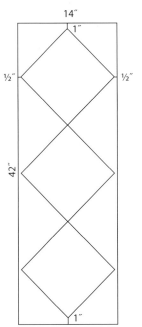

Placement of the diamonds on the background fabric

3. Blanket stitch the diamonds to the background.

4. Following the manufacturer's directions, iron the strip of heavy interfacing to the inside top of the backing fabric, ½" from the top and sides.

5. Pin the background and the backing fabrics with wrong sides together.

6. Fold each piece of twill tape in half, and pin with the raw edges between the backing and the background at the top of the piece. The twill loops should be ¼" from each side and the raw edges should be ½" inside.

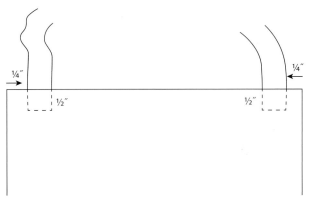

Placement of the twill tape hangers

7. Cut out the wool scallop pieces using the pattern (pullout page P5).

8. Insert the wool scallop between the background and the backing fabric at the bottom.

9. Blanket stitch all the way around the outside of the piece. Make sure to go back and stitch the back of the twill tape hangers and the back of the wool scallop.

10. Add the embellishment stitches as desired to the wool scallops at the bottom.

A STITCHER'S APRON

Techniques: Wool appliqué and embroidery

Finished apron: 19″ × 21½″ (50″ wide with ties)

Working with fabric is a messy business. Happily, the mess is more linty than dirty, but it can present problems for even the tidiest of stitchers. This apron is designed to keep you clean and keep your sewing essentials at hand.

Rebekah had the initial idea: an apron to wear while teaching to hold her extra scissors, notions, and phone. After many requests, and with the help of a talented seamstress, Rebekah made many aprons available for students to purchase and personalize. Now she has created this updated design so that you can make your own apron! This project will walk you through making the linen apron, a wool-appliqué scissor pocket, and an embroidered needle flap.

I personally would have never had a reason to wear this apron five years ago. Paper, ink, and paint were my mediums; I had no interest in sewing. Watching everyone stitch away while on a trip with my mother, I decided to raid the scrap basket and try a little appliqué. The appliqué part was all right, but I found I really enjoyed the decorative embroidery stitches. Several hours of online stitching tutorials later, I was stitching away, and I have not stopped!

This project is a great way to try out a little embroidery work in cotton and wool to go with your appliqué projects.

—*Kelsey*

Photo by Rebekah L. Smith

We share many interests, and we both enjoy sharing our love of stitching.

A stitcher's apron
is a stitcher's friend.

MATERIALS

Apron

- 1 gray linen rectangle 23″ × 18″ for apron base

- 1 gray linen rectangle 7″ × 9½″ for apron pocket

- 1 gray linen rectangle 10″ × 11½″ for apron flap

- 1 natural linen rectangle 5½″ × 88½″ for apron waistband

- -

hint *To conserve fabric, you could piece together the waistband with 3 linen rectangles measuring 5½″ × 29½″ each.*

- -

- 4 pieces of ¼″-wide twill tape, each 23″ long

Apron scissor pocket

- 1 medium-pink wool rectangle 6″ × 7″ for pocket backing

- 1 light-brown wool rectangle 6″ × 5″ for pocket background

- 1 dark-pink wool rectangle 2″ × 3″ for 2 flower petals

- 1 light-pink wool square 3″ × 3″ for 2 flower parts

- 1 antique-white wool square 2″ × 2″ for flower

- 1 black wool rectangle 1″ × 2″ for flower center

- 1 mustard wool square 2″ × 2″ for lower flower petals

- 1 green wool square 2″ × 2″ for 2 leaves

- Embroidery floss: 1 skein each of dark brown (DMC 3371), dark mustard (DMC 829), and antique white (DMC 841)

- Freezer paper (such as Quilter's Freezer Paper Sheets by C&T Publishing)

Apron needle flap

- 1 natural linen rectangle 9″ × 7″ for embroidery background

- 1 medium-pink wool rectangle 8″ × 6″ for embroidery border

- 1 fusible embroidery stabilizer rectangle 9″ × 7″

- Freezer paper (such as Quilter's Freezer Paper Sheets by C&T Publishing)

- Rustic Wool Moire thread: 1 spool of dark green (410)

- Embroidery floss: 1 skein each of chartreuse (DMC 371), dark pink (DMC 632), light pink (DMC 3859), antique white (DMC 841), and dark brown (DMC 3371)

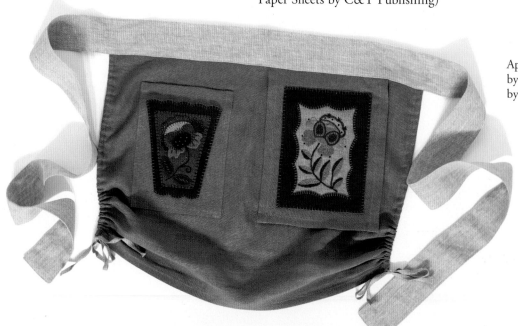

Apron design and wool appliqué by Rebekah L. Smith, embroidery by Kelsey Anilee Smith

APRON

Making Your Project

1. Turn the bottom of the 23″ × 18″ gray linen rectangle for the apron base under ¼″. Press. Turn the bottom under ½″ and press again.

2. Sew a hem along the bottom of the apron.

3. Turn the 2 sides of the apron base under ¼″ and press. Turn the 2 sides under ½″ and press again.

4. Sew a hem along both sides of the apron base.

- -

hint *Be sure not to stitch too close to the edge of the apron. You will need these to be casings for the tapes to gather the sides of the apron.*

- -

5. Turn the sides and the bottom of the 7″ × 9½″ gray linen pocket rectangle under ¼″. Press.

6. Turn the top of the pocket under ¼″ and press. Turn the top under ½″ and press again.

7. Stitch along the top of the pocket.

8. Turn the sides and bottom of the 10″ × 11½″ gray linen flap rectangle under ¼″. Press. Turn the sides and bottom under ½″ and press again. Stitch around the sides and bottom of the flap.

9. Following the placement guide, pin the flap to the apron base along the top of the apron.

10. For each side of the apron, put a safety pin at the top of 2 of the twill tapes, work your way up the inside of the apron's side seam, and pin into place at the top of the apron. Remove the safety pin.

11. Turn the long sides of the waistband under ¼″ and press. Turn each short end under ¼″. Press.

12. Fold the waistband in half lengthwise, with the turned sides to the inside. Press.

13. Pin the waistband to either side of the top of the apron, overlapping the top ½″. Be sure the top of the flap and the top of the tapes are inside the waistband.

14. Stitch the waistband along all 4 sides.

15. Referring to the placement guide (below left), pin the linen pocket to the apron and stitch into place along the 2 sides and the bottom.

16. Press the apron.

17. Gather the tapes to the desired height on the apron after the pocket and needle flap are attached. See the photo (previous page) for the suggested height.

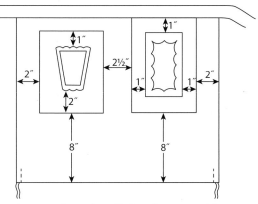

Apron pocket and needle flap placement guide

APRON SCISSOR POCKET

Materials Prep

Refer to How to Wool Appliqué (page 77) as needed for additional details on these steps.

1. Cut out the wool appliqué pieces using the pattern (page 24).

2. Lay out the wool project to be sure you have all the pieces.

Making Your Project

Refer to Stitching Your Projects (page 80) as needed for additional details on these steps.

Note: Stitch only on the light-brown pocket background.

1. Stitch the flower to the light-brown pocket background, working on the pieces in order from the back to the front. Stitch the leaves.

2. Add the embellishment stitches as desired.

3. Turn on the wrong side and press with a steam iron on the wool setting.

4. Pin the finished pocket background to the medium-pink pocket backing. Stitch into place.

5. Turn on the wrong side and press with a steam iron on the wool setting.

Finishing

1. Pin the finished scissor-pocket appliqué to the linen pocket on the apron.

2. Stitch the finished appliqué to the pocket, making sure to leave the top open for your scissors.

----

hint *Slide a piece of card stock inside the apron pocket to keep from stitching it closed.*

Wool-appliqué apron scissor pocket

APRON NEEDLE FLAP

Materials Prep

Refer to How to Embroider (page 78) as needed for additional details on these steps.

1. Transfer the embroidery pattern (page 25) to the natural linen.

2. Following the manufacturer's instructions, iron the embroidery stabilizer to the back of the linen.

3. Cut out the wool appliqué frame using the pattern.

Making Your Project

Refer to Stitching Your Projects (page 80) for details on embroidery stitches.

Stitch the pattern using the stitch guide (below). All wool sections are stitched with 2 strands of thread, and all embroidery floss sections are stitched with 3 strands.

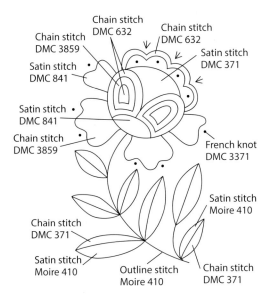

Embroidery stitch guide

1. Stitch the stem and leaf shadows using a double strand of the wool thread. Stitch the cotton floss section of the leaves after you have finished the wool section.

2. Stitch the flower, beginning by stitching the inner petals and then moving outward.

3. Add the embellishment stitches as desired.

Embroidered apron needle flap

Finishing

1. Place the finished embroidery on a towel facedown. Steam press on the wool setting until the linen is flat. Be careful not to crush the embroidery by pressing too hard or ironing faceup.

2. Pin the wool frame securely to the linen, and blanket stitch around the inside only.

3. Turning the piece over, trim the linen so that it is ¼" smaller than the wool on all sides.

4. Pin the embroidered piece to the flap on the apron.

5. Blanket stitch around the outside of the frame to attach the piece to the apron flap.

Gather the tapes to give the apron a fuller look.

Wool-appliqué scissor pocket pattern

Embroidered needle flap pattern

ALL-IN-ONE BASKET

Techniques:
*Wool appliqué •
Embroidery*

Finished basket covers: 19″ × 19″

I love baskets—just ask Kelsey. I am always on the lookout for the next basket, old or new. Even more fun for me is modifying a basket for a project. Baskets have endless uses around the house: hiding ugly things, providing visible storage, or adding texture to a room.

When I was designing this project, I knew I wanted to use a basket. Kelsey and I came up with the idea for a project basket. We always need a basket for storing our in-process work— something we don't use to store threads and needles, just a nice place to lay out projects that are not quite done. I had the basket hand made just for this project, and then I designed a simple cover to protect the pieces inside from dust, dirt, and light. The covers add a decorative element to this storage piece. The beautiful handmade top could also be used to hide books, magazines, or unsightly objects in your homes.

There are two cover options. My Wool Appliqué Cover (page 28) features large flowers blooming on a trellis background, echoed by the windowpane cotton base. Kelsey's Embroidered Cover (page 30) leans more toward the monochrome, with smaller—and more easily embroidered— flowers and leaves.

—*Rebekah*

One of the many uses for my baskets is garden work, a hobby I share with Kelsey.

Photo by Tessa Christine Smith

Try two variations on a theme: one in appliqué and one in embroidery.

Wool Appliqué Cover

MATERIALS

- 1 antique-white wool square 9″ × 9″ for background

- 1 brown wool rectangle 9″ × 15″ for trellis branches

- 1 orange wool rectangle 7″ × 12″ for 3 large flowers and 4 flower buds

- 1 antique-white wool rectangle 4″ × 6″ for flower petal centers

- 1 dark-orange wool rectangle 1½″ × 3½″ for flower centers

- 1 green wool rectangle 4″ × 6″ for 7 leaves

- 1 brown print square 19½″ × 19½″ for front of basket cover

- 1 brown linen square 19½″ × 19½″ for back of basket cover

- Freezer paper (such as Quilter's Freezer Paper Sheets by C&T Publishing)

- Sewing machine

Wool-appliqué basket cover by Rebekah L. Smith.

Getting Started

Refer to How to Wool Appliqué (page 77) as needed for additional details on these steps.

1. Cut out the wool appliqué pieces using the patterns (pullout pages P1 and P4).

2. Lay out the wool project to be sure you have all the pieces.

3. Lay the lattice branches on the antique-white background wool in an interwoven pattern before stitching, as shown (below).

Making Your Project

Refer to Stitching Your Projects (page 80) for details on the blanket stitch and embroidery stitches.

1. Using the blanket stitch, appliqué all the wool pieces to the antique-white background. Start with the lattice pieces and then add the flowers and leaves.

2. Add the embellishment stitches as desired.

3. Using a steam iron on the wool setting, press the finished piece on the wrong side.

Making the Cover

1. Using the basket cover pattern (pullout page P1), make 2 freezer-paper templates of the basket cover. Tape the 2 templates together along the center dotted line, and use this to cut the front of the basket cover. Repeat this with the linen fabric to cut the back of the cover.

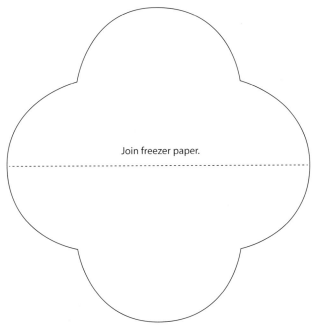

Making the freezer-paper pattern for the cover background

2. Pin the 2 basket cover pieces right sides together.

3. Machine sew around the edges, using a ¼″ seam allowance and leaving an opening of approximately 4″ along the bottom for turning.

4. Turn the basket cover right sides out and press.

- -

hint *Before turning the basket cover, notch carefully around the curved parts to get a nice clean curve.*

- -

5. Pin together the opening and carefully whipstitch (page 85) the opening closed.

Finishing

1. Center the finished appliqué piece onto the top of the basket cover. Blanket stitch into place through both layers of the cover.

2. On each of the rounded flaps of the basket cover, appliqué an orange bud and a green leaf. Add the embellishment stitches as desired.

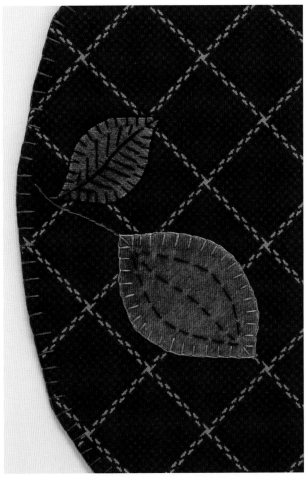

Detail of the appliqué motifs on the basket cover flaps

3. Blanket stitch all the way around the outer edge of the basket cover.

Embroidered Cover

MATERIALS

- 1 linen square 12″ × 12″ for background

- 1 embroidery stabilizer square 12″ × 12″ for background

- 1 burgundy cotton square 19½″ × 19½″ for front of basket cover

- 1 gray floral cotton square 19½″ × 19½″ for back of basket cover

- Rustic Wool Moire thread: 1 spool each of burgundy (785), tan (705), and medium green (231)

- Embroidery floss: 1 skein each of dark pink (DMC 632) and antique white (DMC 841)

- Freezer paper (such as Quilter's Freezer Paper Sheets by C&T Publishing)

- Sewing machine

Getting Started

Refer to How to Embroider (page 78) as needed for additional details on these steps.

1. Transfer the embroidery pattern (pullout page P1) to the natural linen.

2. Following the manufacturer's instructions, iron the embroidery stabilizer to the back of the linen.

Making Your Project

Refer to Stitching Your Projects (page 80) for details on embroidery stitches.

1. Stitch the pattern using the embroidery stitch guide (below). All wool sections are stitched with 2 strands of thread, and all embroidery floss sections are stitched with 3 strands.

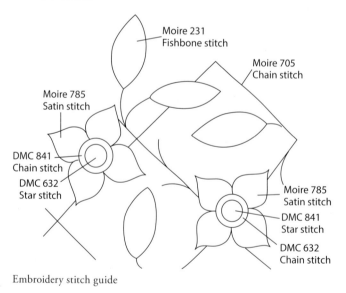

Embroidery stitch guide

Embroidered basket cover by Kelsey Anilee Smith

2. Stitch the wool sections of the flowers; then add the embroidery floss embellishments.

3. Stitch the leaves. Finish by stitching the latticed branches.

Finishing

1. Using a steam iron on the wool setting, press the finished piece on the wrong side. Place a towel underneath the piece to keep from crushing the embroidery.

2. Trim and press to make a ½″ hem all the way around the cotton square.

3. Make the basket cover, referring to the instructions in Making the Cover (page 29).

4. Using a sewing machine, topstitch ¼″ around the whole cover.

5. Center the finished embroidered piece onto the top of the basket cover and blanket stitch it into place.

6. Add the embellishment stitches as desired around the center embroidery. Stitch the featherstitch around the outside edges of the basket cover flaps.

Detail of the embroidered flowers and leaves

NIGHT VOYAGE

Techniques: Wool appliqué and rug hooking

Finished wallhanging: 19″ × 28″

You might be surprised to know that I am a member of a local rug-hooking guild. Though I do very little rug hooking, the ladies let me join anyway, and I stitch away while they hook. It's a fun time, working and chatting, and it's hard not to walk out with a new friend.

This is where I met Cindy Sullivan. Though our friendship began at the guild, we went on to spend many a day out in our favorite local town. These outings always include lunch at the best little café in Chagrin Falls, followed by browsing boutiques and antique shops.

All this exposure to rug hooking, which many appliqué lovers also do, has inspired me to branch out into this area for design. And, of course, I had to throw some appliqué in there. Cindy is one of those friends who can practically read your mind, which made working on this project with her a joy. Her rug hooking captured exactly what I had in mind for the design!

—*Rebekah*

Lunching at Lemon Falls, our favorite café

Photo by Tessa Christine Smith

*This is a great project to combine
two favorite techniques for wool.*

MATERIALS

Wool appliqué

- 1 light antique-white wool rectangle 7″ × 10″ for sail 2 and 1 sail center

- 1 antique-white wool rectangle 7″ × 9″ for sail 3 and 1 sail center

- 1 dark antique-white wool rectangle 7″ × 10″ for sail 1, 1 sail center, and 1 small circle

- 1 blue wool rectangle 5″ × 23″ for waves and 1 extra-large, 1 large, 1 medium, and 1 small circle

- 1 mustard wool rectangle 3″ × 6″ for 2 large circles and 1 small circle

- 1 red wool square 5″ × 5″ for 1 extra-large, 1 large, 1 medium, and 1 small circle

- 1 blue-green wool square 3″ × 3″ for 1 extra-large circle

- 1 dark-mustard wool rectangle 2″ × 4″ for 1 medium and 1 small circle

- 1 dark-blue wool rectangle 2″ × 4″ for 1 medium and 1 small circle

- Fiberfill polyester stuffing

- Embroidery floss: 1 skein each of dark brown (DMC 3371), dark mustard (DMC 829), and antique white (DMC 841)

- Freezer paper (such as Quilter's Freezer Paper Sheets by C&T Publishing)

Rug hooking

- 1 rug-hooking linen rectangle 27″ × 36″

- Various dark-blue wool rectangles totaling 44″ × 70″ for night sky

- 1 antique-white wool rectangle 10″ × 14″ for flag stripes, stars, moon, and border circles

- 1 red wool rectangle 5″ × 25½″ for flag stripes, border circles, and banner

- 1 dark-brown wool rectangle 8″ × 4″ for mast lines, circles, thin borders, and flag outline

- 1 blue wool rectangle 10″ × 34″ for foreground, waves, and border circles

- 1 blue-green wool rectangle 22″ × 26″ for midground sea and border circles

- 1 gold wool rectangle 5″ × 16″ for hull stripe and border circles

- 1 dark-gold wool rectangle 36″ × 40″ for hull and border background

----

hint   *Cut ⅜″-wide strips for the black border and cut ¼″-wide strips for the rest of the project. (If you are using a strip cutter, it would be a #9 cut for the black border and a #8 cut for the rest of the project.)*

- 96″ length of 1″-wide twill tape

Design and wool appliqué by
Rebekah L. Smith, rug hooking
by Cindy Sullivan

WOOL APPLIQUÉ

Getting Started

Refer to How to Wool Appliqué (page 77) as needed for additional details on these steps.

1. Transfer the pattern (pullout page P2) to the rug-hooking linen.

----

hint *Draw all the motifs—even those that are for wool appliqué only—as this will help with laying out the project.*

----

2. Use the same pattern to cut out the wool appliqué pieces (pullout page P2).

3. Lay out the wool project to be sure you have all the pieces.

MAKING YOUR PROJECT

Refer to Stitching Your Projects (page 80) for details on the blanket stitch and embroidery stitches.

1. Blanket stitch the sails into place. Leave a 2″ opening on one of the sides and add fiberfill.

----

hint *Be sure not to overfill the wool appliqué pieces that get the fiberfill. They should be just lightly full.*

----

2. Stitch shut the openings.

3. Stitch the waves into place, leaving a 2″ opening at the top and bottom of each wave.

4. Add the fiberfill to the waves and stitch shut the openings.

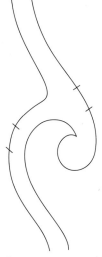

Leave openings to add fiberfill to the waves.

5. Repeat this process with each of the wool appliqué circles on the border, adding fill beneath the largest circle in each set.

6. Add the embellishment stitches as desired.

RUG HOOKING

Making Your Project

Refer to How to Rug Hook (page 86) as needed for additional details on these steps.

1. Hook the black outline around the center.

2. Hook the hull of the ship, along with the mast details.

3. Hook the ocean and flags and then the sky.

4. To finish the border, hook the black outline around the outside.

5. Finish by hooking the circles and the border background.

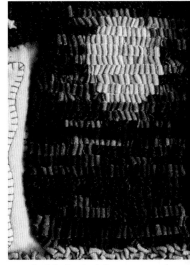

Detail of the hooked sky

Finishing

1. Turn the rug onto the wrong side. Using a damp towel covered with a piece of muslin or cotton, press with an iron on the wool setting.

----

hint *A steamer works best if you have access to one.*

----

2. Trim the rug-hooking linen, leaving a 1″ hem allowance.

3. Turn under the rug-hooking linen and cover with the twill tape. Pin into place.

4. Whipstitch (page 85) the twill tape on both sides.

HEARTFELT

Technique:
1. *Wool appliqué*
2. *Rug hooking*

Finished wallhanging[1]: 9½″ × 11″ • Finished ottoman[2]: 9″ × 14″

I am always on the lookout for beautiful materials to use in my creations. While on the hunt for hand-dyed wool, my mother and I stumbled across Donna Bennett. Little did I know that a friendship would be born, with much collaboration to follow!

Donna's rug hooking is beautiful, and she is a wonderful teacher. We have participated in many events together, and we always have a good time. She is one of the best dyers I know, creating beautiful colors for any wool project.

These projects were especially fun to design because I was able to make the wool appliqué pattern for the Wool Appliqué Wallhanging (page 38) and the rug hooking pattern for the Rug-Hooked Ottoman (page 39) exactly the same. Even though the visual design is the same, you can end up with two very different looks and final products. I hope you try them both, especially if you are a dabbling creative. If not, maybe you'll make a matching set with a friend, like I did, to add a little heart to your home.

—*Rebekah*

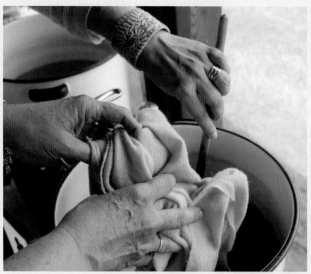

Photo by Rebekah L. Smith

Donna and I teach a wool-dyeing and appliqué class together every year.

*Make a set of matching hearts
for your home.*

Wool Appliqué Wallhanging

MATERIALS

- 1 antique-white wool rectangle 11″ × 11″ for large heart background

- 1 black wool rectangle 8″ × 11″ for 6 large scallops

- 1 light-green wool rectangle 7″ × 10½″ for 6 medium scallops and 2 leaves

- 1 green wool rectangle 5″ × 8″ for 6 small scallops and 2 leaves

- 1 red wool rectangle 1½″ × 3″ for 2 circles

- 1 black wool rectangle 11″ × 11″ for backing

- Embroidery floss: 1 skein each of dark brown (DMC 3371), dark mustard (DMC 829), and antique white (DMC 841)

- 30″ length of ⅜″-wide double-fold bias binding

- 24″ length of ribbon or twill tape for bow and hanger

- Freezer paper (such as Quilter's Freezer Paper Sheets by C&T Publishing)

Wallhanging by
Rebekah L. Smith

Getting Started

Refer to How to Wool Appliqué (page 77) as needed for additional details on these steps.

1. Cut out the wool appliqué pieces using the pattern (pullout page P4).

----

hint *Add some extra length to your freezer-paper patterns for the second and third row of scallops and the leaves for the overlap.*

----

2. Lay out the wool project to be sure you have all the pieces.

Making Your Project

Refer to Stitching Your Projects (page 80) for details on the blanket stitch and embroidery stitches.

1. Using the blanket stitch, appliqué all the wool pieces to the heart background.

2. Add the embellishment stitches as desired.

Detail of the wool-appliqué heart

3. Using a steam iron on the wool setting, press the finished piece on the wrong side.

4. Pin together the finished heart and the backing heart.

- -

hint *To help keep everything aligned, you may want to baste together the two pieces.*

- -

5. Pin the bias binding around the outside edge of the heart, starting at the bottom point.

6. Once you have gone all the way around, turn under ½″ of the bias binding and overlap the piece at the bottom point.

7. Whipstitch (page 85) the binding all the way around the heart on both the front and the back.

8. Tie a bow in the center of the ribbon / twill tape. Knot together the 2 ends.

9. Stitch the bow to the center of the top of the heart.

Rug-Hooked Ottoman

MATERIALS

- ⅛ yard of light green, medium green, and antique-white wool
- ¼ yard of black wool
- ⅛ yard of red wool

- -

hint *Cut ³⁄₁₆″-wide strips for the heart and details and ¼″-wide strips for the background and outer border. (If you're using a strip cutter, use a #6 cut for the ³⁄₁₆″ strips and a #8 cut for the ¼″ strips.)*

- -

- 1 rug-hooking linen square 22″ × 22″
- 1 decorator-weight cotton rectangle 10½″ × 46″ for ottoman base
- 1 batting rectangle approximately 6″ × 43″ (Size may vary. See Hint, at right.)
- 1 paper square 13″ × 13″ for bottom of ottoman
- 1⅜ yards of 1½″-wide twill tape
- 1⅜ yards of 2¼″-wide jute ribbon

Ottoman design by Rebekah L. Smith, rug hooking by Donna Bennett

- 1⅜ yards of heavy twine or braid
- 1 round papier-mâché box with lid, 14″ in diameter
- Nonflammable contact cement or tacky glue
- 1″ foam brush

- -

hint *The size of the batting may vary. You will need to measure your box to be sure.*

- -

Getting Started

Refer to How to Rug Hook (page 86) as needed for additional details on these steps.

1. Transfer the pattern (pullout page P4) to the rug-hooking linen.

2. Cut some of the wool strips to get the center motif started. Continue to cut strips as needed as you hook your project.

Making Your Project

1. Hook the red outline of the heart.

2. Starting with the bottom scallop, hook in the dark green; then hook in the light green and the black. Do this for each of the scallops, working your way up the piece from the bottom.

3. Hook the flowers and leaves; then fill in the white background of the large heart. Finish the center motif with the white outline and red heart at the top.

4. Hook the outside border in red to frame the piece and keep the circle uniform.

5. Fill in the remaining black background.

Finishing

1. Baste the cotton batting together around the base of the box.

2. Press a ½″ hem along one short side of the decorator cotton.

3. Wrap the decorator cotton around the box and batting, and pin in place with the hemmed side overlapping. There should be extra fabric overhanging the top and bottom evenly.

4. Blanket stitch down the side of the cotton.

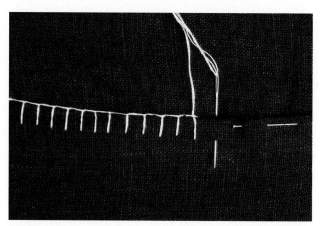
Stitching the ottoman sides

5. Cut slits in the overhanging fabric around the bottom of the ottoman.

6. Using the nonflammable contact cement or tacky glue and following the manufacturer's directions, glue the overhanging cotton to the bottom of the ottoman base. The fabric sections will overlap a bit.

Gluing the edges over the ottoman bottom

7. Glue the top overhanging linen to the inside of the box; then glue the twill tape over the cut edges of the linen. Fold under the end of the tape ½″ and glue it neatly over the beginning of the tape. Let the glue dry for several hours.

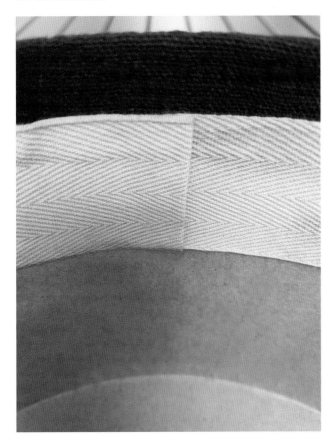

8. Glue the jute ribbon around the side of the box lid. To glue the jute ribbon to the top of the box lid, simply add glue to the top edge of the lid and press the jute ribbon over, making small folds in the ribbon on the top of the lid. Let the glue dry for several hours.

9. Cut a 12″ circle out of the paper, and glue it to the bottom of the box.

10. Trim around the finished hooked top, leaving 2″ of linen.

11. Notch the linen all the way around the circle.

12. Turn under and press into place.

13. Determine the placement of the rug on top of the box lid. Whipstitch (page 85) it to the jute ribbon all the way around.

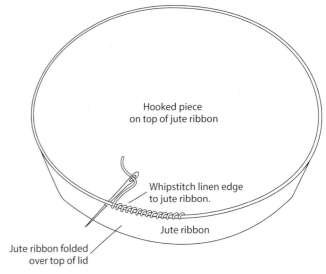

Hooked piece on top of jute ribbon

Whipstitch linen edge to jute ribbon.

Jute ribbon

Jute ribbon folded over top of lid

14. Glue the heavy twine into place, filling in the space between the hooked piece and the edge of the box lid.

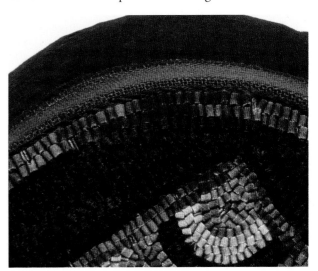

NESTING

Technique:
1. Wool appliqué
2. Dimensional wool

Finished pillow[1]: 11" × 17" • Finished nested bluebird[2]: 5" × 4"

Lori Ann Corelis is a dear friend who is also my partner for several events. Together, we put on a folk art show and a stitching retreat. Having met through our own businesses, we have become more than business partners. We always enjoy sitting down to talk shop, life, and more.

Lori Ann is known best for her wonderful mohair animals. I wanted to include something dimensional in this book, and Lori Ann is the one you call to think in 3D. She created this delightful little Dimensional Wool Nested Bluebird (page 46) on a pincushion nest. I made a Wool Appliqué Pillow (page 44) to coordinate.

—*Rebekah*

Photo by Tessa Christine Smith

Lori Ann and I have worked together before, combining our love of folk art and textiles to create events and sometimes even artwork.

Make these happy little bluebirds to bring a little outdoors in.

Wool Appliqué Pillow

MATERIALS

- 1 brown tweed-wool rectangle 11″ × 17″ for background

- 1 light-mustard wool rectangle 4″ × 11″ for tree limb A and baby bird

- 1 mustard wool rectangle 8″ × 10″ for tree limb B, tree limb C, and baby bird wing

- 1 dark-mustard wool rectangle 4½″ × 10″ for tree limb D

- 1 blue wool rectangle 4″ × 8″ for bird and 3 eggs

- 1 dark-brown plaid wool rectangle 4½″ × 8″ for nest

- 1 brown wool rectangle 2″ × 6″ for nest center

- 1 dark-brown wool square 2½″ × 2½″ for wing

- 1 dark-orange wool rectangle 2″ × 3″ for wing

- 1 orange wool rectangle 3″ × 2″ for bird head and wing

- 1 light-green wool rectangle 3″ × 5″ for 3 leaf centers

- 1 green wool rectangle 5″ × 9″ for 3 large leaves and 6 small leaves

- 2 natural linen rectangles 12″ × 18″ for pillowcase

- Embroidery floss: 1 skein each of dark brown (DMC 3371), dark mustard (DMC 829), and antique white (DMC 841)

- Freezer paper (such as Quilter's Freezer Paper Sheets by C&T Publishing)

- 11″ × 17″ pillow form

Wool appliqué pillow by Rebekah L. Smith

Getting Started

Refer to How to Wool Appliqué (page 77) as needed for additional details on these steps.

1. Cut out the wool appliqué pieces using the pattern (pullout page P3).

2. Lay out the wool project to be sure you have all the pieces.

Making Your Project

Refer to Stitching Your Projects (page 80) for details on the blanket stitch and embroidery stitches.

1. Using the blanket stitch, appliqué all the wool pieces to the tweed background.

2. Add the embellishment stitches as desired.

3. Using a steam iron on the wool setting, press the finished piece on the wrong side.

4. Center the finished piece onto 1 linen rectangle and blanket stitch it into place.

5. Pin the 2 linen rectangles right sides together.

6. Machine sew around the edges, using a ½″ seam allowance and leaving an opening (approximately 12″) along the bottom for turning and inserting the pillow.

7. Turn the piece right side out and insert the pillow form.

8. Pin together the opening and carefully whipstitch the opening closed.

----

hints

- *To allow for a flatter pillow, remove up to one-third of the fill from the pillow form before inserting it.*

- *For easy insertion, fold the pillow in half and carefully insert it into the cover.*

Detail of the embellishment stitching

Dimensional Wool Nested Bluebird

By Lori Ann Corelis of The Spotted Hare

MATERIALS

- 1 brown wool rectangle 7″ × 14″ for nest
- 1 blue wool rectangle 6″ × 9″ for bird and eggs
- 1 soft-red wool rectangle 3″ × 6″ for bird's breast
- 1 rust wool square 1″ × 1″ for beak
- 2 black beads 4 mm for eyes
- 8″ length of 9/16″-wide crinkle ribbon for bow around bird's neck
- Wool threads for decorative stitching: Genziana 12-weight wool thread in blue (498) and cinnamon (448)
- Embroidery floss for decorative stitching: Valdani size 12 in red brown (1641) and spruce green (833)
- Valdani size 8 wool thread for wrapping tuffet: Black (8122)
- Sewing thread
- 1 brown card stock square 4″ × 4″ for base
- Heavy buttonhole or carpet thread in medium brown and black
- Liquid seam sealant (such as Fray Check)
- Fiberfill polyester stuffing
- Permanent craft adhesive
- 1 doll needle 3″–4″ long
- 4 or 5 long corsage pins
- 2 large heavy washers 2½″ across with ¾″ opening for weight
- Tweezers
- Pinking shears

Nested bluebird by Lori Ann Corelis

Getting Started

Refer to How to Wool Appliqué (page 77) as needed for additional details on these steps.

1. Cut out the wool pieces using the patterns (page 49).

2. Lay out the wool to be sure you have all the pieces.

Making the Nest

Refer to Stitching Your Projects (page 80) for details on the embroidery stitches.

1. On 1 nest circle only, cut a 2″ slit, centered. This will be used for turning in a later step.

2. Pin the 2 nest circles with right sides together. Sew completely around, using a ¼″ seam allowance. Clip the curves.

3. Turn the nest through the opening from Step 1, making sure the curves are turned out nicely. Stuff firmly but not hard.

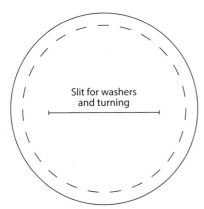

Cutting the slit to insert the washers in the nest

4. Insert 2 large washers, stacked upon each other, into the bottom slit so they lie flat. This will give your pincushion a nice weight. Whipstitch the opening closed with heavy thread. You will cover this spot later.

5. Embroider a featherstitch along the nest side seam. Add French knots to the tip of each "feather" with a thread that matches the bird's breast.

6. To make the nest into a tuffet, use 1½ yards of Valdani size 8 wool thread and a doll needle. Knot well at the center bottom of the tuffet. Insert the needle up through the tuffet, exiting dead center. (You will stitch through the holes in the washers.) Lay the thread over the top of the tuffet and insert the needle from the bottom to the top again.

Continue a total of 4 times to make an X shape, dividing the tuffet in fourths. Repeat 4 times again in an X shape to divide the tuffet in eighths, making 8 sections total to your tuffet. Keep the thread taut to make the tuffet "poof" a bit.

Once the sections are complete, run the thread up and down through the center a few times before knotting off at the bottom to secure well.

7. Pin 2 of the eggs in place about halfway between the center and edge seam of 2 adjacent sections; then pin

1 egg similarly on the other side. Blanket stitch the eggs to the nest with red thread, and add the embellishment stitches as desired.

Making the Bird

1. With right sides together, pin and stitch together the bird sides using the backstitch from point A (the neck) to point B (the tail). Leave the bottom of the bird open.

2. Insert the breast gusset, with the wider end toward the neck, point A. Pin one side and stitch in place, leaving open where noted to stuff. Pin the other side in place and stitch. Leave a 2″ opening for stuffing on one side of the breast. Clip the curves very carefully, and turn right side out. Stuff the bird firmly and stitch the opening closed.

3. With the red decorative thread, featherstitch (page 83) the bird's seams. Pin the wings in place on either side of the body, and blanket stitch them to the bird. Add the embellishment stitches as desired.

Side view of the nested bird

4. Following the manufacturer's instructions, apply liquid seam sealant (such as Fray Check) all over the bird beak to stiffen it. Let dry completely. When dry, fold the beak in half and clamp the folded edge with tweezers for a few minutes. With sewing thread, stitch the beak in place at the front of the head across the center fold of the beak.

5. Use 2 pins to determine the eye placement. Once you are happy, use a heavy black thread to stitch the black beads in place. Stitching through the head from one eye to the other will help the eyes settle nicely into the head.

6. Fold the tail feather piece in half. Trim the edges with pinking shears, making the top "feather" about ¼″ shorter than the bottom one. With red decorative thread, blanket stitch together the sides and folded edge of the tail, and add the embellishment stitches as desired. With regular sewing thread, stitch the tail in place at the top of the bird's behind.

Detail of the back of the bird

Finishing

1. Pin the bird in place on top of the woolen nest with corsage pins to prevent the piece from shifting while stitching. Pay close attention to the direction you would like your bird to face and where her eggs are.

2. With the heavy medium brown thread and a doll needle, knot at the bottom of the nest. (You will be stitching through the center hole of the washers again.) Enter the bottom center of the nest and exit under the bird where the rear belly meets the nest, making sure to catch just a bit of the bird (approximately ½″ across her underbelly). Place the needle back down into the nest and exit the bottom.

Enter the bottom again and come out where the breast meets the nest, again catching just a bit of the bird. Then go back down into the nest and out through the bottom.

Repeat this process about 3 times for each end so that the bird settles nicely into the nest. Knot off securely on the bottom.

3. With pinking shears, cut a 2½″ circle from the brown card stock. Glue it to the bottom of the nest, being careful to keep the glue at least ¼″ from the edge of the card stock piece so you won't have any glue oozing out.

4. Using the crinkle ribbon, tie a bow around the bird's neck.

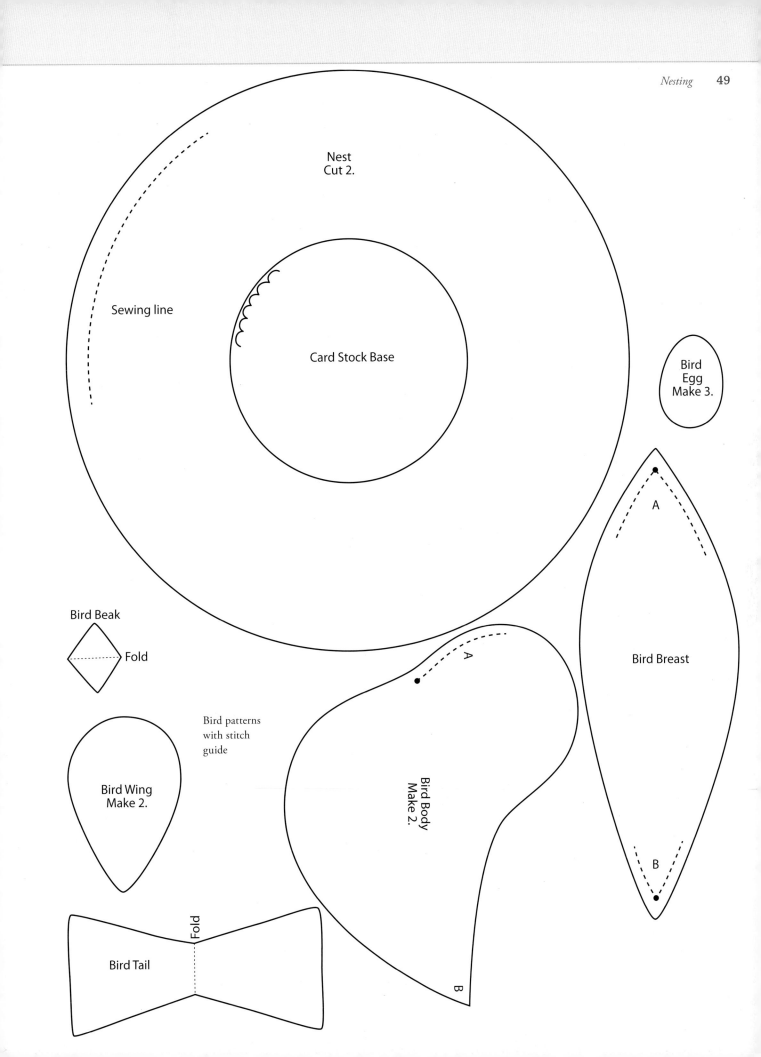

Nest
Cut 2.

Sewing line

Card Stock Base

Bird Egg
Make 3.

A

Bird Breast

B

Bird Beak

Fold

Bird patterns
with stitch
guide

A

Bird Wing
Make 2.

Bird Body
Make 2.

Fold

Bird Tail

Fold

B

SNIP 'N' STITCH

Finished sewing caddy: 9½″ × 8¼″

Let me introduce you to my dear friend Susan Meyers! She is a fellow wool lover from Texas who hooks rugs along with doing punch-needle embroidery and appliqué. Susan and I met when she took a wool appliqué class I was teaching, and we have been friends ever since. We share a love of the Lord, family, and—of course—wool! Every year, I head down to her wool shop to teach classes and spend time with her and her lovely family.

This project uses wool appliqué combined with small quantities of the punch-needle technique. Punch-needle embroidery is similar to rug hooking in its use of closely placed loops to fill an area, but it is usually classified as embroidery because of its miniscule nature.

This technique has a long history (possibly as far back as ancient Egypt!) with various methods, but the basics have changed very little. This little sewing caddy is a great project to get a taste for punch needle and to add extra flair to your wool appliqué.

—*Rebekah*

Photo by Tessa Christine Smith

Susan and I enjoy sharing about our faith and lives when we get together over a cold glass of iced tea—always with lemon!

This little sewing companion will keep all the notions you need for snipping and stitching.

MATERIALS

Punch needle

- 1 weaver's cloth 16″ × 15″

- Embroidery floss (DMC):

    1 skein each:

    Dark green (934) for tree

    Light green (3051) for tree

    Olive green (3011) for tree

    Chartreuse (371) for door/window frames

    Brown gray (3787) for windowpanes

    Dark brown gray (3021) for windowpanes

    Dark brown (3371) for spool and pockets

    Dark pink (632) for spool

    Cranberry red (3857) for spool

    2 skeins each for door/windows and pockets:

    Ecru (612)

    Light brown (611)

    Medium brown (610)

Design and wool appliqué by Rebekah L. Smith,
punch-needle embroidery by Susan Meyers

Wool appliqué

- 1 antique-white wool rectangle 2″ × 6″ for roof

- 1 dark-brown wool rectangle 4″ × 6″
  for 2 scrolls and 2 pockets

- 1 faded-red wool rectangle 2½″ × 5″
  for 2 scrolls and gate

- 1 light-green wool rectangle 4″ × 2″ for tree

- 1 light-brown wool rectangle 6″ × 2″
  for awning and tree trunk

- 1 red wool square 4½″ × 4½″ for shop

- 2 cotton rectangles 10½″ × 9¼″ for
  background and backing

- Embroidery floss (DMC):

    1 skein each:

    Ecru (612)

    Light brown (611)

    Medium brown (610)

- 12″ length of ½″-wide ribbon or twill tape for hanger

- 1 sheet of double-sided fusible

- Fiberfill polyester stuffing

- Freezer paper (such as Quilter's Freezer
  Paper Sheets by C&T Publishing)

PUNCH NEEDLE

Refer to How to Punch Needle (page 90) as needed for additional details on these steps.

1. Trace the pattern (page 54) onto the weaver's cloth, leaving 1″ between each design. These patterns *do not* need to be reversed.

2. Following the color guide (page 54), punch the spool, the pocket fronts, the windows, the door, and the tree.

3. Punch the signs in this order: outline the border, punch the letters of the sign, and then fill in the background.

4. For the spool, once you have outlined it, fill in the dark pink and cranberry red in stripes to mimic threads.

WOOL APPLIQUÉ

Getting Started

Refer to How to Wool Appliqué (page 77) as needed for additional details on these steps.

1. Cut out the wool appliqué pieces using the pattern (page 55).

2. Lay out the wool project to be sure you have all the pieces.

Making Your Project

Refer to Stitching Your Projects (page 80) for details on the blanket stitch and embroidery stitches.

1. Blanket stitch the red rectangle to the background cotton.

2. Pin the awning to the top of the red rectangle, leaving the sides and bottom of the awning loose to make a needle flap.

3. Stitch the rest of the wool pieces on, except for the 2 brown pockets. Note that the roof is a pincushion.

Be sure to leave a 1″ opening to add a small amount of fiberfill; then blanket stitch the opening closed.

4. Add the embellishment stitches as desired.

5. Using a steam iron on the wool setting, press the finished piece on the wrong side.

FINISHING

1. Cut out each finished punch-needle motif, leaving a ¼″ seam allowance of the weaver's cloth all the way around.

2. Turn under the extra weaver's cloth around the punch-needle motifs and tack them down.

---

hint *You may need to notch some of the rounded parts so that they lie flat.*

Detail of finishing the punch-needle pieces

3. Cut a piece of fusible slightly smaller than each of the punch pieces.

4. Following the manufacturer's instructions, adhere the fusible to the back of each of the punched pieces.

5. One at a time, adhere the punched pieces to the project, making sure they are straight. Gently tack down the pieces where needed with a few whipstitches (page 85).

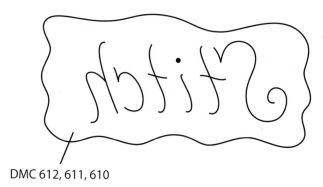

DMC 612, 611, 610

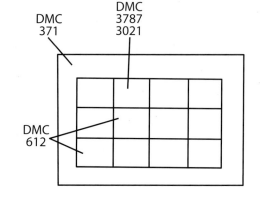

6. To make the Snip 'n' Stitch pockets, stitch the punch-needle pieces onto the wool rectangles.

7. Blanket stitch the pockets into place, leaving the top side open.

8. Using a steam iron on the wool setting, press the finished piece on the wrong side.

9. Press a ½" hem all the way around the front and backing pieces.

10. Pin the front and backing pieces with the wrong sides together.

11. Pin the twill tape hangers 1" from each corner at the top, between the front and backing.

12. Blanket stitch all the way around the piece to finish. Be sure to go back and blanket stitch the back side of the twill tape hangers.

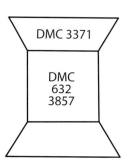

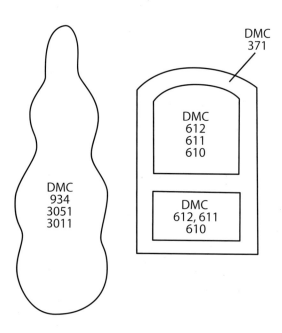

Punch-needle patterns with color guide

DMC 3371

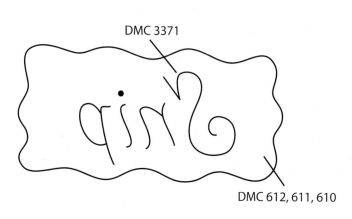

DMC 612, 611, 610

Wool appliqué patterns

LEAPS AND BOUNDS

Technique:
1. Wool appliqué
2. Punch needle

Finished table rug[1]: 19″ × 37″ • *Finished basket[2]:* 6″ × 9″

One fun fact about Susan Meyers is that she lives on a ranch. And it's not a ranch if there are no horses, of course! Though she has a big heart for all animals, the horse is one of Susan's favorites, and she and her husband own several of them. So, of course, when I was designing a punch-needle project for this chapter with her, I knew I had to do a horse motif.

Translating a wool appliqué design into a punch-needle embroidery design was a fun experience. The smaller size required for punch needle allows you to add some finer details, like the little corn kernels or the variegated flowers. Wool appliqué can be very flat sometimes, and punch needle allows you to use color to give dimension. There are lots of threads involved in this project, but the colors will allow you to play around with textures and give some energy to your horse!

Try this design in either the Wool Appliqué Table Rug (page 58) or the Punch-Needle Basket (page 59), or both!

—*Rebekah*

Photo by Tessa Christine Smith

Susan and I had a great time sorting through thread colors for this project.

*Try one design in
two techniques!*

Wool Appliqué Table Rug

MATERIALS

- 1 mustard wool rectangle 7″ × 20″ for 4 cornstalks, 2 sunflowers, and 2 sunflower centers

- 1 dark-mustard wool rectangle 5″ × 10″ for 4 cornstalk tops and 6 corn husks

- 1 black wool rectangle 13″ × 10″ for 2 horses, 4 sunflower centers, and 2 buds

- 1 dark-rust wool rectangle 4½″ × 9″ for 6 corn pieces, 2 sunflowers, 2 sunflower centers, and 2 bud centers

- 1 light-green wool rectangle 7½″ × 12″ for 1 sunflower stem, 3 ground pieces, and 3 leaf centers

- 1 green wool rectangle 7½″ × 12″ for 1 sunflower stem, 3 ground pieces, and 3 leaf centers

- 1 natural linen rectangle 18″ × 36″ for background

- 1 linen or cotton rectangle 18″ × 36″ for backing

- Embroidery floss: 1 skein each of dark brown (DMC 3371), dark mustard (DMC 829), and antique white (DMC 841)

- 2 cotton pieces 3″ × 38″ for binding on long sides

- 2 cotton pieces 3″ × 20″ for binding on short sides

- Freezer paper (such as Quilter's Freezer Paper Sheets by C&T Publishing)

Getting Started

Refer to How to Wool Appliqué (page 77) as needed for additional details on these steps.

1. Cut out the wool appliqué pieces using the pattern (pullout page P3).

2. Lay out the wool project to be sure you have all the pieces. The 3 ground pieces should be 1″ from the edge of the linen background.

Making Your Project

Refer to Stitching Your Projects (page 80) for details on the blanket stitch and embroidery stitches.

1. Pin the 2 cornstalks, the cornstalk tops, the corn, the corn husks, and the 1 flower stem in place as shown.

2. Using the blanket stitch, appliqué these pieces to the background linen.

3. Stitch the sunflowers, leaf centers, and 3 ground pieces.

4. Add the horse.

Wool appliqué table rug by Rebekah L. Smith

5. Repeat Steps 1–4 on the other end of the linen background.

6. Add the embellishment stitches as desired.

Detail of the wool appliqué

Finishing

1. Using a steam iron on the wool setting, press the finished piece on the wrong side.

2. Prepare the binding strips by folding the long edges over ½" to the wrong side. Press. Fold the binding strip in half with the wrong sides together and press again.

3. Layer the finished wool appliqué on top of the backing cotton/linen, and pin together.

4. Pin the long binding strips to each side of the finished appliqué and backing.

5. Pin the short binding strips along each end of the finished appliqué and backing, folding each end under ½".

6. Whipstitch (page 85) the binding into place on the front and the back.

7. Press the binding.

Punch-Needle Basket

MATERIALS

- 1 weaver's cloth 10" × 13"

- 1 jute basket
  9" wide × 9" high × 7" deep

- Nonflammable contact cement

- 1" foam brush

- Embroidery floss (DMC):

  2 skeins each for horse:

  Black (310)

  Charcoal (799)

  Gray (535)

  1 skein each for stems and cornstalks:

  Olive green (3011)

  Chartreuse (371)

  1 skein each for flowers and corn:

  Dark gold (869)

  Gold (680)

  Orange (400)

  Burnt orange (919)

  3 skeins each for background:

  Medium brown (3862)

  Antique white (841)

  Beige (842)

  1 skein each for interior ground:

  Teal (924)

  Dark gray blue (413)

  Gray blue (926)

Design by Rebekah L. Smith, punch-needle embroidery by Susan Meyers

Making Your Project

Refer to How to Punch Needle (page 90) as needed for additional details on these steps.

1. Trace the pattern (next page) onto the weaver's cloth. This pattern *does not* need to be reversed if you want the horse to face left in the finished project.

2. Using an embroidery hoop and following the color guide (next page), begin by punching the border around the edge of the project. The outline will keep the center design from stretching.

3. Outline the horse and punch some guidelines inside the body to form the direction of the stitches.

4. Fill in the horse using a mix of the grays and black.

5. Punch the motifs behind the horse. Start with the stems and move to the leaves and then the flowers.

6. Continue punching, moving on to the variegated corn, followed by the cornstalks.

7. Punch the ground by outlining the inside tongues and outer border. Fill in, starting with the inside tongues and moving to the ground border.

8. Fill in the background.

Finishing

1. Complete the punch-needle rectangle.

2. Trim the weaver's cloth, leaving a ¼″ hem allowance around the finished punch-needle rectangle.

3. With an iron on the cotton setting, press the ¼″ hem allowance to the back of the punch needle.

4. Using the nonflammable contact cement, glue the punch-needle piece to the front of the basket.

5. Place the basket on its side, with the punch needle facing down. Weight the inside with several heavy books to allow the punch-needle piece to dry flat.

Detail of the punch needle

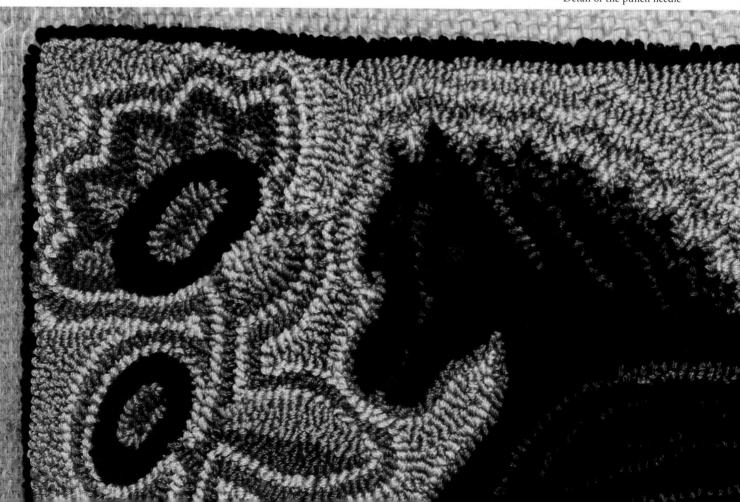

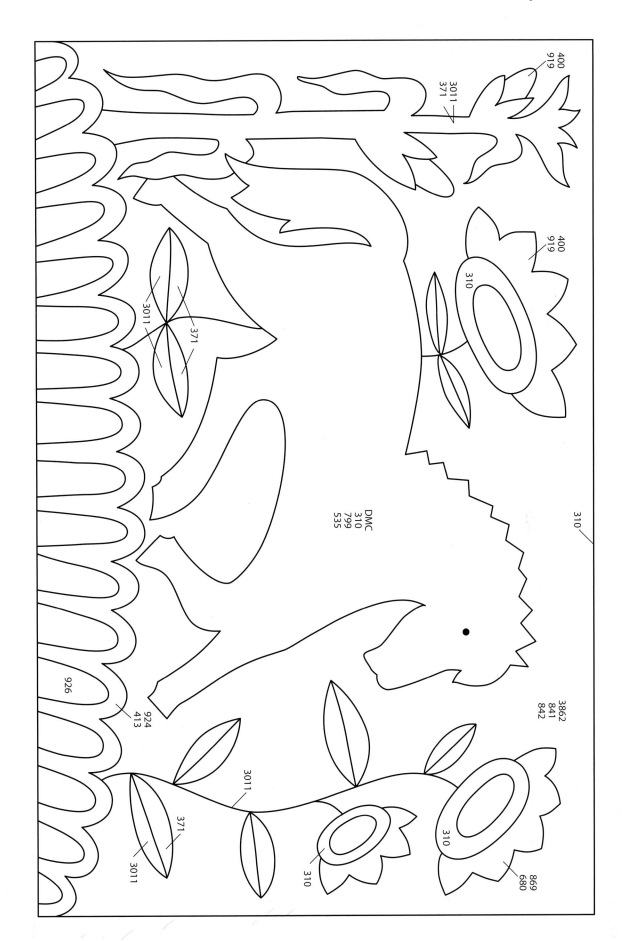

PINWHEEL POSY

Finished table rug[1]: 36″ × 18″ • *Finished pillow[2]: 20″ × 20″*

Kathy Wright, an antiques dealer and textile arts aficionado, has been a longtime family friend. We met through antiques, but our common interests extend beyond that. Kelsey, Kathy, and I volunteered together at the local historical society, cataloging collections, planning events, and staging historic rooms. There's never a quick visit with Kathy—we always have so much to talk about!

Not many people have heard of *yarn sewing*, which predates rug hooking and is sometimes mistaken for it. Traditionally, yarn-sewn items were purely decorative, ranging in use from bedcovers to table rugs, and were meant to add a little beauty to the early home. Some more delicate examples actually use silk thread on a fine linen.

The Yarn-Sewn Pillow (page 66) in this project takes a more folky tone, using heavy wool yarn and a loose-weave linen. It is the perfect project for a beginner in yarn sewing. On the other hand, the wool appliqué version of the design, the Wool Appliqué Table Rug (page 64), is for the more adventurous stitchers who want to try a larger project.

We asked Kathy for her advice about yarn sewing. Famous for her profound "Kathy-isms" (as we call them), she replied, "You can't push a river; just go with the flow." And so it is with yarn sewing!

—*Rebekah*

Photo by Kelsey Anilee Smith

Kathy and I share a love of all things historic and antique.

This table rug and matching yarn-sewn pillow add different wool textures to your home.

Wool Appliqué Table Rug

MATERIALS

- 1 antique-white wool rectangle 12″ × 23″ for 2 large circles, 4 small flowers, and 8 edges

- 1 dark-blue wool square 15″ × 15″ for 1 large circle, 4 small flowers, 4 flower centers, and 8 edges

- 1 dark-red wool rectangle 10″ × 15″ for 4 small flowers, 8 flower centers, and 8 edges

- 1 light-green wool rectangle 10″ × 11″ for 4 large leaves and 2 leaf centers

- 1 green wool rectangle 9″ × 10″ for 2 large leaves and 4 leaf centers

- 1 dark-red linen rectangle 19″ × 37″ for background

- 1 linen rectangle 19″ × 37″ for backing

- Embroidery floss: 1 skein each of dark brown (DMC 3371), dark mustard (DMC 829), and antique white (DMC 841)

- 3⅛ yards of linen rickrack for trim

- Freezer paper (such as Quilter's Freezer Paper Sheets by C&T Publishing)

Wool appliqué table rug by Rebekah L. Smith

Getting Started

Refer to How to Wool Appliqué (page 77) as needed for additional details on these steps.

1. Cut out the wool appliqué pieces using the pattern (pullout page P5).

2. Lay out the wool project to be sure you have all the pieces.

Making Your Project

Refer to Stitching Your Projects (page 80) for details on the blanket stitch and embroidery stitches.

1. Using the blanket stitch, appliqué all the wool pieces to the background linen.

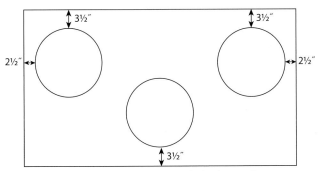

Placing the large circles on the background

2. Add the embellishment stitches as desired.

3. Using a steam iron on the wool setting, press the finished piece on the wrong side.

4. Iron a ½″ hem all the way around the linen background.

5. Pin the rickrack trim to the back of the hem with only the top half showing.

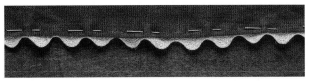

Pinning the rickrack edging

6. Blanket stitch or whipstitch the rickrack edging all the way around the piece.

7. Iron a ½″ hem all the way around the backing linen.

8. Pin the backing linen to the finished piece. Blanket stitch or whipstitch all the way around, attaching the backing linen to the rickrack edging.

Detail of the wool appliqué

Yarn-Sewn Pillow

MATERIALS

- 1 rug-hooking linen square 17″ × 17″

- Tapestry needle

- 630 yards of red hand-dyed wool yarn

- 369 yards of natural off-white wool

- 220 yards of dark blue yarn

- 123 yards of dark green yarn

- 210 yards of light-green hand-dyed yarn

- 1⅝ yards of ½″-wide twill tape

- 20″ × 20″ finished pillow in a complementary color

Design by Rebekah L. Smith, yarn sewing by Kathy Wright

Making Your Project

Refer to How to Yarn Sew (page 88) as needed for additional details on these steps.

1. Trace the pattern (pullout page P5) onto the rug-hooking linen.

2. Stitch the large center-motif details; then move outward, stitching the circles.

3. Stitch the leaves, starting with the centers. Once the centers are filled in, stitch the leaf borders.

4. Stitch 1 row of the outline to stabilize the piece and keep the inside background stitches from distorting the project edge. Fill in the background, starting in the center and moving out from there.

Finishing

1. Turn the rug onto the wrong side. Using a damp towel covered with a piece of muslin or cotton, press with an iron on the wool setting.

2. Trim the rug-hooking linen, leaving a 1″ hem allowance.

3. Turn under the rug-hooking linen and cover with the twill tape. Pin into place.

4. Whipstitch (page 85) the twill tape on both sides.

5. Using a lot of pins, pin the piece to the pillow, making sure it is straight and centered.

- -

hint *It is helpful to tack down each corner first to keep the piece from shifting as you sew it.*

- -

6. Use a coordinating thread to whipstitch the piece to the pillow.

A GARDEN PATCHWORK

Techniques:
Wool appliqué
and quilting

Finished table rug: 23″ × 23″

Kathy Wright is a wealth of information, especially about textiles. I have to give her credit for teaching me the freezer-paper method for cutting out my wool appliqué patterns. She dabbles in most textile arts, but making quilts and quilting are among her passions.

I meet a great number of quilters who enjoy working in wool appliqué. Quilting has its own appliqué process, of course, but I can see how so many people enjoy both quilting and wool appliqué.

Because of this, I knew I would have to design a project for quilters who also love appliqué. Kathy made a tiny quilt for the center, using cottons and a black linen. I framed the simple geometric center with a bold floral motif in appliqué. If you don't quilt already, this basic piece could be a great first step.

—*Rebekah*

Photo by Tessa Christine Smith

Kathy and I love all things textiles, from threads to fabrics.

Combine a quilt
and appliqué for a
unique table mat.

MATERIALS

Wool appliqué

- 1 black wool square 23″ × 23″ for background

- 1 red wool rectangle 11″ × 11″ for
  6 tulips and 8 flower centers

- 1 green wool rectangle 11″ × 17″ for
  6 leaves and 6 tulip bands

- 1 light-green wool rectangle 10″ × 8″ for 6 medium
  leaf centers and 8 medium flower petals

- 1 black wool rectangle 4″ × 7″ for 6 small leaf centers

- 1 tan wool rectangle 7″ × 6″ for 8 large flower petals

- 1 black wool/felt rectangle 23″ × 23″ for backing

- Embroidery floss: 1 skein each of dark
  brown (DMC 3371), dark mustard (DMC 829),
  and antique white (DMC 841)

- Freezer paper (such as Quilter's Freezer
  Paper Sheets by C&T Publishing)

Quilt

- 1 black linen rectangle 17½″ × 5″ *or* 1 strip 2½″ × 36

- 1 faded red cotton square 6″ × 6″

- 1 green cotton square 5″ × 5″

- 1 mustard cotton square 5″ × 5″

- 1 tan cotton square 5″ × 5″

- Sewing machine

fabric note   The cotton used in the quilt is
Aged Muslin by Marcus Fabrics. The variegated
colors in these cottons help give the center quilt
depth and dimension.

Design and wool appliqué by
Rebekah L. Smith, center quilt
by Kathy Wright

QUILT

Making Your Project

1. Cut out the following:

- 13 squares 2½″ × 2½″ from the black linen

- 3 squares 2½″ × 2½″ *each* from the green, mustard, and tan cotton

- 4 squares 2½″ × 2½″ from the faded red cotton

2. Cut each square in half diagonally to make 2 triangles.

3. Make units by sewing together 1 black linen triangle and 1 cotton triangle on the longest side, right sides together and using a ¼″ seam.

4. Lay out all the units as shown in the project photo (previous page).

5. Sew together the individual units to make 5 rows.

Sewing a row

6. Sew together the rows to form the quilt center.

7. Turn under the outer edges and press. Center the patchwork in the middle of the wool background and use a small whipstitch (page 85) to attach it to the background.

WOOL APPLIQUÉ

Getting Started

Refer to How to Wool Appliqué (page 77) as needed for additional details on these steps.

1. Cut out the wool appliqué pieces using the patterns (pullout page P3).

2. Lay out the wool project to be sure you have all the pieces.

Detail of the wool appliqué

Making Your Project

Refer to Stitching Your Projects (page 80) for details on the blanket stitch and embroidery stitches.

1. Using the blanket stitch, appliqué all the wool pieces to the background wool.

2. Add the embellishment stitches as desired.

3. Using a steam iron on the wool setting, press the finished piece on the wrong side.

4. Pin together the finished appliqué and the backing fabric.

5. Blanket stitch all the way around the outside edge.

A PLACE FOR PIECES

*Techniques:
Wool
appliqué and
cross-stitching*

Finished folio cover: 13″ × 14″ closed • 13″ × 28″ open

Many of you who have read my past books have read about how I started stitching. The credit for this goes to my mother, Christine Miller, an excellent stitcher. This project takes a look at another common interest my mother and I share: books. This folio cover is a kind of book, bound and filled, and so it seemed an appropriate project to collaborate on with her.

This oversized folder gives you a large space to lay out and keep your project pieces without them sliding around. My mother's fine cross-stitching makes a wonderful binding for this project, which is meant to be both useful and beautiful. You might also use the folio cover to hide loose papers on a desk or cover other items around the house.

I have many memories of sitting around the kitchen table, everyone reading together. Popcorn, a genetically passed-down craving in my family, was a common treat. From classics to histories to books about historic folk art, my mother passed a love of reading on to me and to my own children.

—*Rebekah*

Photo by Tessa Christine Smith

For my mother and me, reading practically requires a bowl of good popcorn.

*Find a place for all
the loose pieces and
parts of a project that
is in progress.*

MATERIALS

Wool appliqué

- 1 tan wool rectangle 10″ × 7″ for background

- 1 antique-white wool rectangle 3″ × 5″ for top center

- 1 black wool rectangle 6″ × 7″ for top and small scallops at bottom

- 1 green wool rectangle 4″ × 7″ for stem

- 1 red wool rectangle 3½″ × 9″ for large heart and large scallops

- 1 mustard wool square 2″ × 2″ for small heart

- Embroidery floss: 1 skein each of dark brown (DMC 3371), dark mustard (DMC 829), and antique white (DMC 841)

- Freezer paper (such as Quilter's Freezer Paper Sheets by C&T Publishing)

Cross-stitch

- 1 sampler linen (28-count) rectangle 19″ × 15″

- Embroidery floss: 1 skein each of brown gray (DMC 3787), red (DMC 3721), dark olive green (DMC 730), and mustard (DMC 783)

Folio

- 2 red linen squares 14″ × 10½″ for cover

- 1 natural linen rectangle 14″ × 23″ for cover

- 2 medium-weight chipboard squares 12″ × 12″ for cover inserts

- Sewing machine

WOOL APPLIQUÉ COVER

Getting Started

Refer to How to Wool Appliqué (page 77) as needed for additional details on these steps.

1. Cut out the wool appliqué pieces using the pattern (pullout page P3).

2. Lay out the wool project to be sure you have all the pieces.

Making Your Project

Refer to Stitching Your Projects (page 80) for details on the blanket stitch and embroidery stitches.

1. Using the blanket stitch, appliqué all the wool pieces to the tan background.

2. Add the embellishment stitches as desired.

3. Using a steam iron on the wool setting, press the finished piece on the wrong side.

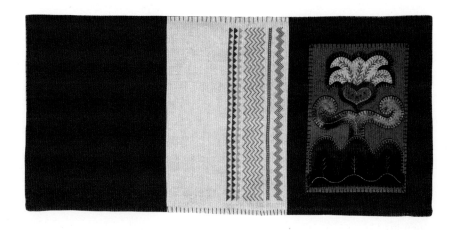

Made by
Rebekah L. Smith,
cross-stitched binding
by Christine Miller

CROSS-STITCH BINDING

Making Your Project

Refer to Stitching Your Projects (page 80) for details on counted cross-stitch.

When starting the cross-stitch pattern, make sure to leave a border of 3″ on the right-hand side and top, leaving plenty of blank space on the left side for the back of the binding. To help you count, you can mark your borders with pins or draw a chalk line.

1. Stitch the cross-stitch, using the pattern and color guide (at right). Use 2 strands of floss.

2. Trim the cross-stitched binding so that it measures 14″ high × 9″ wide, with a 1″ border on the right side and 1½″ on the top and bottom sides. Leave a 4½″ border to the left of your stitching.

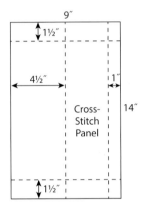

Trim the cross-stitched panel.

FOLIO COVER

1. Machine stitch the sampler rectangle to both linen squares along the long edges, right sides together and using a ½″ seam allowance.

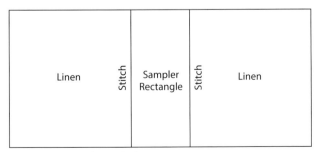

Stitching the sampler to the linen

2. Press open the seams.

3. Align the folio cover with the natural-linen folio interior, right sides together. Pin securely.

4. Machine stitch all the way around the 2 sides and the top, using a ½″ seam allowance and leaving the bottom open.

5. Center the finished appliqué onto the red linen and pin.

6. Blanket stitch the appliqué to the cover, being careful not to stitch through the interior fabric.

7. Insert chipboard pieces from the bottom, positioning them so they are ¼″ away from the outside edges.

8. Turn under the bottom edge of the cover and the interior edge of the cover ½″. Pin shut.

9. Blanket stitch along the outside edge of the cover.

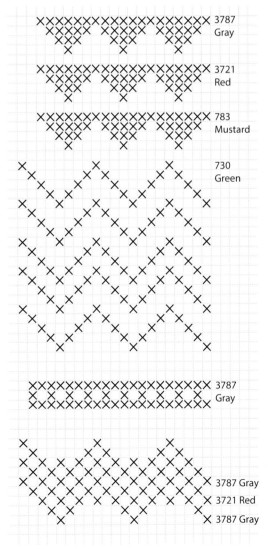

Cross-stitch patterns with color guide

TECHNIQUES
FOR WOOL

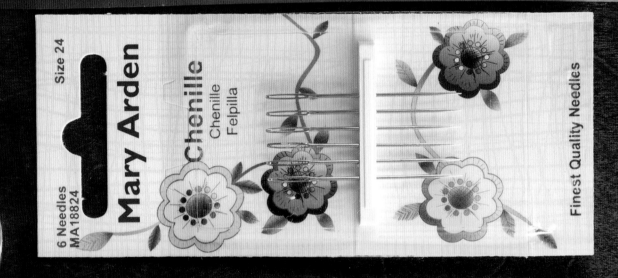

HOW TO WOOL APPLIQUÉ

Along with your threads, you will need the following supplies:

- Freezer paper (such as Quilter's Freezer Paper by C&T Publishing)

- Chenille #24 needles

- Pins

- Ultrafine permanent marker

- Ruler

- Pencil

- Scissors

1. Measure the wool for the background. Cut it according to the dimensions given in the materials list for each project.

2. Trace the pattern pieces onto the dull side of the freezer paper and cut them out on the traced lines. (You may want to make multiples of the same shape, or you can use the same freezer-paper pattern several times.)

3. Place the freezer-paper pattern pieces onto the appropriate wool, shiny side down. Set your iron for wool, and iron the freezer-paper pattern pieces onto the wool. Space them close together for best use of the fabric.

Iron the freezer-paper patterns securely to the wool.

4. Cut around the freezer-paper pattern attached to the wool, making sure you have all the pieces needed for the project.

5. Keep the wool pieces organized in a plastic bag or multiple bags, and set them aside until you are ready to stitch.

6. Lay out all the wool pieces on the background.

7. Pin only the bottommost layer of wool pieces to the background first. I always stitch the bottom layer to the background first and then add the next layer or layers.

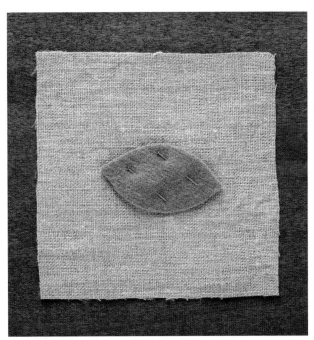

Pin the wool shape to the background.

See Stitching Your Projects (page 80) for instructions on the blanket stitch, which is used to stitch all the wool pieces on, and other stitches for embellishment.

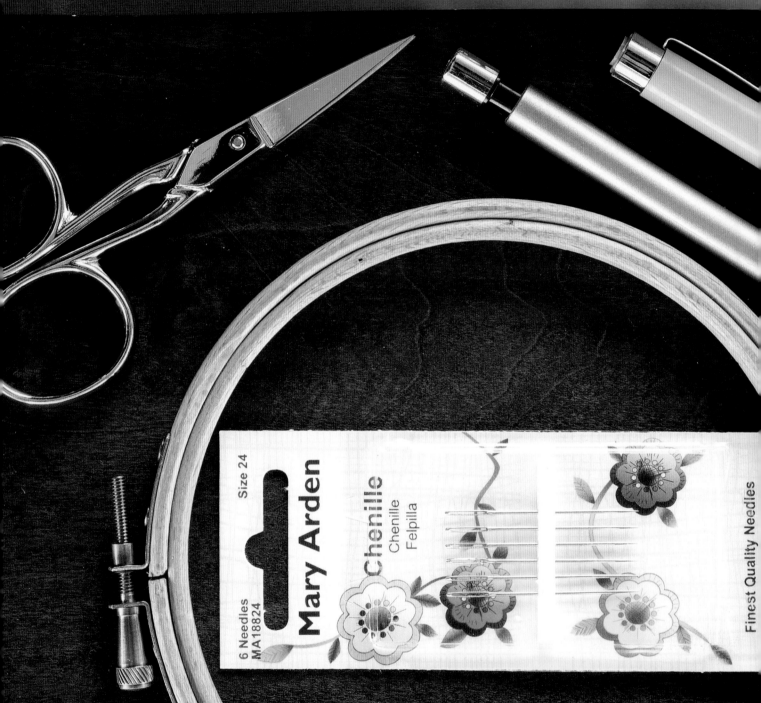

HOW TO EMBROIDER

Along with your threads, you will need the following supplies:

- Freezer paper (such as Quilter's Freezer Paper Sheets by C&T Publishing)

- Chenille #24 needles

- Embroidery hoop

- Ultrafine permanent marker

- Ruler

- Pencil

- Scissors

- Iron

- Lightbox or window

1. Trace the pattern onto the dull side of a piece of freezer paper cut to the pattern size. Make sure to reverse the pattern when you trace it onto the freezer paper.

2. Cut out the background fabric. Make sure there is room for a 3″ border around the pattern so that you have good tension in your embroidery hoop.

3. Center the freezer-paper pattern on the wrong side of the fabric. Iron in place, using the wool setting on your iron.

4. Turn your piece over and place it on a lightbox or window. Using an ultrafine permanent marker, carefully trace the pattern onto the fabric. Once the pattern is drawn, remove the freezer paper.

5. Cut a piece of embroidery stabilizer to the size of the project. Following the manufacturer's directions, adhere the stabilizer to the back of the project.

You are ready to stitch!

See Stitching Your Projects (page 80) for instructions on specific stitches used to embroider.

STITCHING YOUR PROJECTS

The following stitches are used throughout various projects in the book. They are listed in alphabetical order. All projects use a double strand of cotton floss for stitching unless otherwise noted.

Backstitch

1. Knot the thread and bring the needle up at point A; then insert it down at point B.

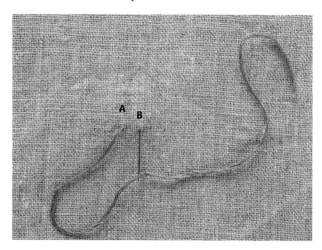

2. Bring the needle up at point C and insert it down at point B.

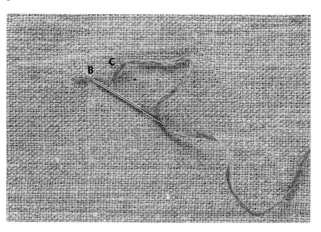

3. Continue to make a series of stitches in a row, keeping them consistent in length.

Blanket Stitch

The blanket stitch is used to appliqué wool shapes to a background. Through her teaching, Rebekah has learned that each person has a natural rhythm to the stitching and an individual stitch length. Strive for consistent, even stitches, somewhere between ⅛″ and ¼″ long.

1. Knot the end of the floss. Bring the needle and floss up through the background, right next to the piece you want to stitch.

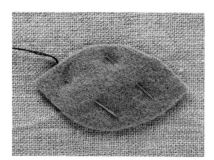

2. Holding the piece you are stitching vertically, insert the needle down through the background 1 stitch length away along the edge of the appliqué. Bring the needle up through the 2 layers, 1 stitch length in from the edge.

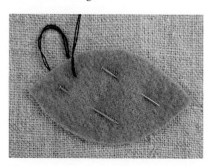

3. Pull the floss through until you have a small loop at the side.

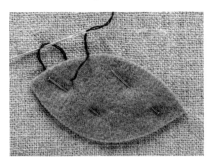

4. Insert the needle through the loop and draw the floss snug against the appliqué piece.

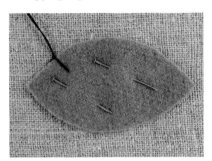

5. Repeat Steps 2–4 all the way around the piece. Repeat Step 1 as needed for any additional pieces and when you need to start a new length of thread.

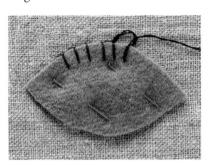

---

helpful hints *When you need to start a new length of floss, stop stitching at the outer edge after making a stitch into the appliqué. Insert the needle to the wrong side and knot off. Begin stitching inside the previous stitch by bringing the needle up through the background at a right angle. This will hide the stopping and starting points.*

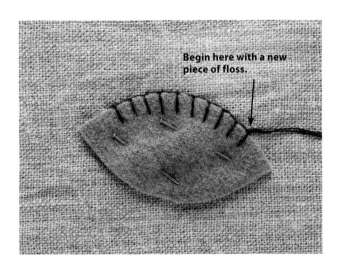

Begin here with a new piece of floss.

To make a crisp corner, insert the needle through the background at the point. Then bring the needle back up again, next to where the needle went down, to anchor the stitch at the point.

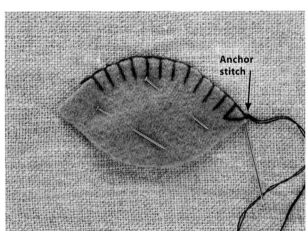

Anchor stitch

Blanket Stitching Outer Edges

The blanket stitch is also used to finish the raw edges of a wool piece.

1. Knot the floss and come up through the wrong side of the wool, 1 stitch length in from the raw edge. Trim the thread tail close to the knot.

2. Catch a bit of the fabric at the edge, as shown; make a loop with the floss; and pull the needle through the loop.

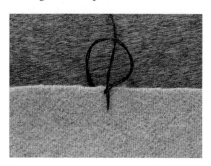

3. Insert the needle into the wool, 1 stitch length away, and bring the needle up through the loop of thread. Draw it up snugly but not too tight. Refer to Blanket Stitch, Steps 4 and 5 (page 81).

4. To make a crisp corner on the outside, make a tiny stitch at the point and take the needle through the loop to create a knot. Anchor the next stitch.

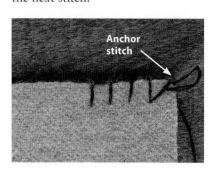

Chain Stitch

1. Knot the thread and bring the needle up through the fabric at point A.

2. Leaving a loop of thread in the direction of point B, insert the needle at point A and come up through point B. Catch the loop with the thread coming out of point B.

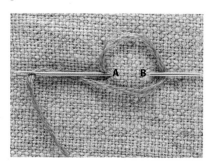

3. Repeat Steps 1 and 2 so that each stitch holds the previous loop in place. To finish, tack down the last loop. Coming up at point B, catch the loop and go back down through point C.

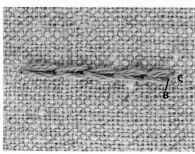

helpful hints

Filling in: *When filling in a shape with the chain stitch, make sure to outline the shape first. Then stitch toward the inside of the shape in concentric rows of stitches. Make sure the chain stitch continues to go in the same direction around the inside of the shape, and stitch until filled.*

Stitching: *When stitching a shape in the chain stitch, be careful not to pull your stitches too tight, as this will cause the fabric to pull and not lie flat. If you pull a stitch too tight, you don't have to pull it out. Simply loosen it with your needle and adjust the tension.*

Cross-Stitch

1. Knot the thread and bring the needle up through the fabric. Insert the needle back down to make an angled stitch.

2. Bring the needle up again and continue to make a series of stitches at an angle.

3. Make diagonal stitches in the opposite direction to finish the crosses.

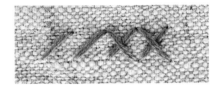

- -

hint *When using cross-stitch linen to do counted cross-stitch, use the weave of the fabric to make even, straight stitches. Count 2 holes over from point A and then 2 holes up to determine where point B is. Do the same in the opposite direction to make your X.*

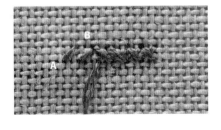

- -

Featherstitch

1. Knot the thread and bring the needle up through the fabric at point A.

2. Insert the needle at point B, bringing it up through the fabric at point C. Catch the thread between points A and B with the needle.

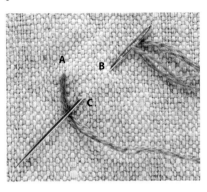

3. Insert the needle down at point D, bringing it up through the fabric at point E. Catch the thread between points A and B with the needle.

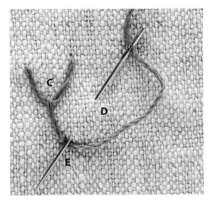

4. Repeat Steps 1–3 until you have stitched as far as you want. Try to keep the center stitches in a straight line to keep it looking neat.

Fishbone Stitch

1. Knot the thread and bring the needle up at point A. Insert the needle down at point B.

2. Bring the needle up at point C and insert at point D.

3. Repeat Steps 1 and 2, using the outline to determine where point A and C are until you have filled in the shape. Add a straight stitch where you started to make the leaf point.

French Knot

1. Knot the floss and bring the needle up through the fabric where you want the French knot. Wrap the floss around the needle 5 times.

2. Push the wraps together and toward the point of the needle.

3. Insert the needle down through the fabric, right next to where you came up. Holding on to the wraps with the thumb of your non-sewing hand, pull the needle through to the other side. This will create a round knot on the surface.

Outline Stitch

1. Knot the floss and bring the needle up through the fabric at point A. Insert the needle down at point B and up at point C, about halfway between points A and B. Pull the thread through to make a stitch. Insert the needle down again at point D and up next to point B for the second stitch.

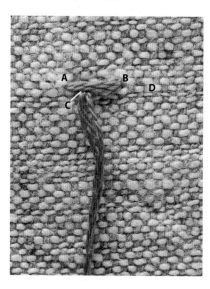

2. Repeat the stitch until you have stitched as far as you want. Keep the stitches even and keep the thread below the line of stitching.

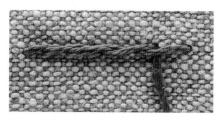

hint To stitch text or other complex designs on light wool, mark the wool using a fine-point felt-tip marker and stitch with a darker floss. If you want to mark a design on dark fabric, try using a chalk marking pencil in a light color.

Running Stitch

1. Knot the floss and bring the needle up through the fabric. Insert the needle back down to the wrong side and up again to make the stitch.

note **Gathering stitch:** A running stitch using larger stitches

2. Insert the needle back down and continue to make a series of stitches in a row. Keep the stitch length even and consistent.

Satin Stitch

1. Use the backstitch (page 80) to outline the shape you will be filling in.

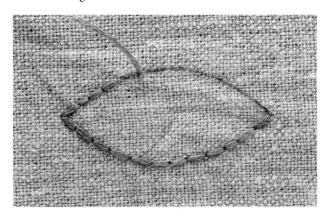

2. Use closely placed straight stitches to fill in the shape. Be sure to cover up the backstitch guidelines.

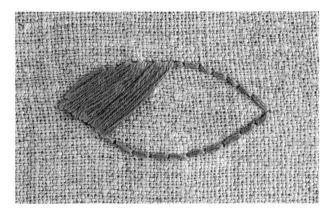

Stars

1. Knot the floss and bring the needle up through the fabric where you want the center of the star. Insert the needle back down through the fabric to make a stitch. This first stitch will determine the size of the star.

2. Repeat the stitch, coming up near the same center hole. Take a stitch in the opposite direction and then 2 stitches at a 90° angle to make a plus sign (+) or an *X*.

3. Take a stitch between each of the 4 stitches until you have made a total of 8 to create the star.

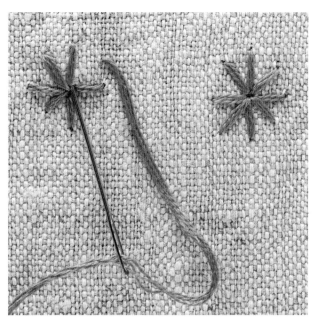

Whipstitch

1. Knot the floss and bring the needle up through the fabric. Insert the needle back down to make an angled stitch.

2. Bring the needle up again and continue to make a series of stitches at an angle. These can be close together to close an opening or farther apart to create a design.

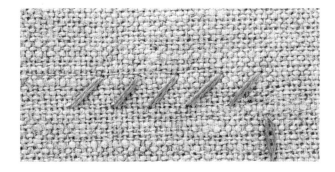

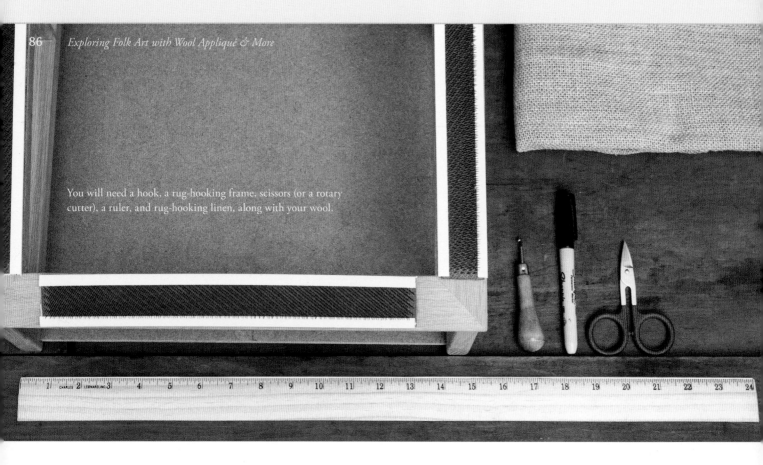

You will need a hook, a rug-hooking frame, scissors (or a rotary cutter), a ruler, and rug-hooking linen, along with your wool.

HOW TO RUG HOOK

Preparing Your Materials

1. Cut the background linen, making sure to allow for 4″ extra all the way around the pattern.

2. Measure and mark several dots 4″ in on each side using a permanent felt-tip marker.

3. **For a straight-sided pattern:** Draw a straight line in the ditch of the linen on each side to create the border of the pattern.

For a circular pattern: Use the dots to center the pattern on the linen.

4. Place the linen onto a lightbox or window. Trace the pattern onto the rug-hooking linen using a fine-point felt-tip pen.

5. Using scissors or a rotary cutter, cut the wool into the widths indicated. You can also use a rug-hooking strip cutter.

Photos by Tessa Christine Smith

Drawing in the ditch of the linen

Hooking Your Project

All the projects in this book use a primitive hook.

1. Pull the linen tight on the rug-hooking frame. You will need the tension to pull the loops through.

2. Hold the first wool strip underneath. From the top, use the hook to pull one end all the way through to the top.

3. About every 2 holes, pull up a loop, making sure that the loops all stay a consistent height.

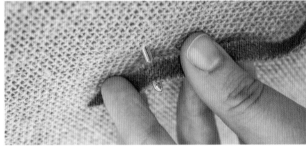

Holding the wool strip underneath

4. Continue pulling the loops up until you reach the end of the strip. Pull the end up through to the top and leave it.

5. To start the next strip, pull up the new end in the same hole that the last strip ended in (if the pattern allows).

6. Continue hooking, using the colors indicated, until the pattern is filled in. Trim the ends that stick up flush with the loops. To finish, see the individual project instructions.

----

hint *For more in-depth instructions, see the book* Introduction to Rug Hooking *by Kris Miller (Ampry Publishing, LLC).*

Photos by Tessa Christine Smith

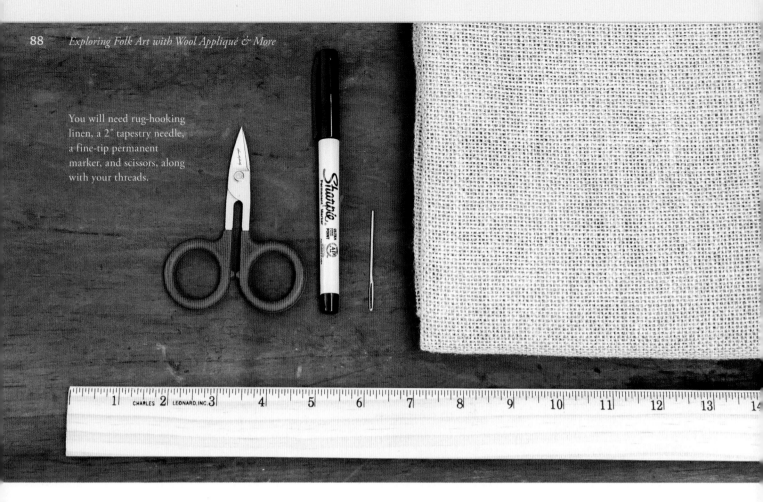

You will need rug-hooking linen, a 2″ tapestry needle, a fine-tip permanent marker, and scissors, along with your threads.

HOW TO YARN SEW

Preparing Your Materials

The yarn-sewing project in this book uses rug-hooking linen. See the instructions for preparing the pattern in How to Rug Hook, Preparing Your Materials (page 86).

Sewing Your Project

1. Thread about 2′ of yarn onto a tapestry needle.

2. Starting on the top, insert the needle into the corner or one side of the area you want to fill. Pull the thread until a 1″ tail remains on top.

3. Hold the tail toward the middle of the area you are filling, and bring the needle back up, right next to where you went down.

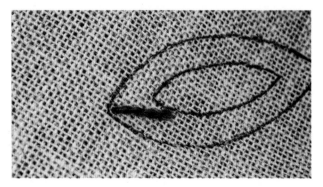

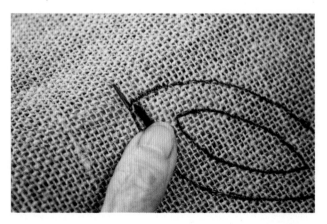

Photos by Tessa Christine Smith

4. Begin to cover the tail with even stitches, using the line as a guide. Keep the stitches at an even length.

5. To tie off, make a stitch down on the back. Thread the needle through some of the previous threads and cut the thread off.

6. Once you have finished, check over the piece for blank spots and fill them in. To do this, secure the end of the yarn by threading it under a portion of the stitching on the back. Come up through the linen, fill in the gap, and secure the thread the same way as before, trimming the ends. To finish, see the individual project instructions.

helpful hints

Deep curves: *Compensate for the curve so that the yarn fills the background. Don't be afraid to go into the same hole with your thread to fill in a blank spot and create a smooth curve line.*

Yarn sewing curves

Stitch sizes: *The tighter the stitches, the more yarn you may need. The stitches may not always be completely even because of the weave of the fabric and the parts of the design. This is not a problem as long as you keep them within a certain size range to create a consistent look.*

Photos by Tessa Christine Smith

You will need a large embroidery hoop, a needle punch, a fine-tip permanent marker, and scissors, along with your threads.

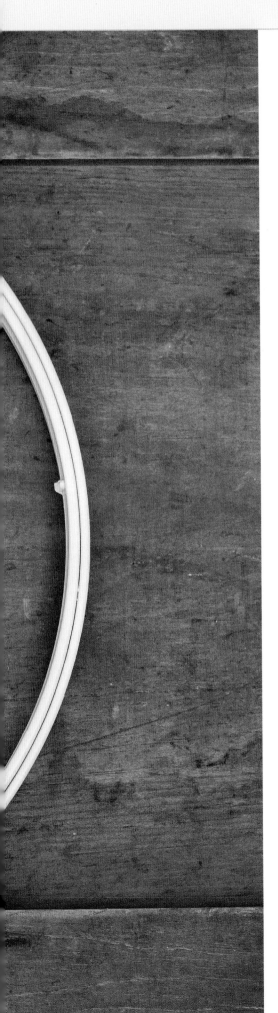

HOW TO PUNCH NEEDLE

Preparing Your Materials

1. Cut a piece of weaver's cloth 3″–4″ larger than your project, making sure it is big enough to be put in an embroidery hoop.

2. Reverse the pattern and trace it onto the weaver's cloth using a lightbox or window.

3. Put the weaver's cloth into the embroidery hoop with the reversed pattern on top. You will work from the *back* of the piece.

Punching Your Project

1. Thread your punch needle according to the manufacturer's directions. Thread with a whole skein rather than cutting a length of thread, and trim once you are done with the section you are working on.

2. Insert the needle through the weaver's cloth until the needle just comes out the other side. Pull the needle back up through the cloth, move over slightly, and repeat. Make sure to punch close together, but be sure not to punch in the same hole as any other stitch.

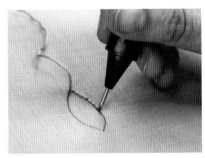

3. To change colors, put the point of scissors on the top of the last loop punched. Hold it down and pull the needle and thread back until there is enough room to clip the thread.

4. Continue punching until you have filled in the whole project. To finish, see the individual project instructions.

Photos by Tessa Christine Smith

GALLERY

This book is the product of friendship and collaboration, and our creative community, near and far, is very dear to us. We are fortunate to have friends who were excited to bring their designs and expertise to our book, whether they collaborated with us on the projects or made their own versions of our projects in their own styles.

The gallery of projects (below) features alternate colorways, designs, and project types of the book's projects by some of our friends.

The gallery of friends (page 94) shows the friends who collaborated with us on the projects in this book. We couldn't have done it without them!

Gallery of Projects

Photo by Alexander Gagliardi

Patti Gagliardi and Jill Zartler are a mother-daughter stitching team who began as Rebekah's students and have become dear friends. They made their versions of the All-in-One Basket (page 26).

Terry Hedrick and Deb Tomsheck are fellow rug-hooking friends who keep Rebekah and Kelsey laughing. They made their versions of Heartfelt (page 36).

Debbie Gulland is a fellow wool appliqué enthusiast who began with rug hooking. She made pillows using the appliqué block from Wallhanging Garden (page 12).

Ginger Jackson and Pati Wolfe are textile arts enthusiasts with many talents. Together they made their version of A Garden Patchwork (page 68).

Gallery of Friends

Cindy Sullivan and Rebekah L. Smith worked together on Night Voyage (page 32).

Donna Bennett and Rebekah L. Smith worked together on Heartfelt (page 36). Visit Donna at Crows on the Ledge (crowsontheledge.com).

Lori Ann Corelis and Rebekah L. Smith designed their coordinating projects in Nesting (page 42). Visit Lori Ann at The Spotted Hare (thespottedhare.com).

Susan Meyers and Rebekah L. Smith worked together on Snip 'n' Stitch (page 50) and Leaps and Bounds (page 56). Visit Susan on Facebook at The Shepherd's Wool and Antiques or visit her shop in Wichita Falls, Texas.

Kathy Wright and Rebekah L. Smith worked together on Pinwheel Posy (page 62) and A Garden Patchwork (page 68).

Christine Miller and Rebekah L. Smith worked together on A Place for Pieces (page 72).

ABOUT THE AUTHORS

Rebekah L. Smith

Antiques have been a part of Rebekah Smith's life from an early age. She grew up surrounded by people who appreciated the simple lines and bold colors of early American folk art.

Rebekah graduated from the Art Institute of Pittsburgh with a degree in graphic design. It was Rebekah's mother who challenged her to paint on a cupboard in the style of early American muralist Rufus Porter, saying, "Try it, and you can keep it." Rebekah has never stopped painting on old surfaces. She has studied Rufus Porter's style and Pennsylvania German folk art, both of which continually inspire her work. She also enjoys working on interiors, painting murals, and stenciling.

Rebekah's woolwork was inspired by a photo of an early American child's bedcover appliquéd with animals. Rebekah interpreted this piece into a reality for her youngest daughter. It was her first wool project and resulted in a new, textile-based inspiration. She now repurposes wool and hand dyes it, using a combination of natural and commercial dyes. Rebekah's passion lies in color and design, both talents that are well suited to folk art.

She and her husband, along with their three daughters, continually work to restore their 1838 house in the Western Reserve of Ohio.

Visit Rebekah online and follow on social media!
Website: rebekahlsmith.com
Facebook: /RebekahLSmithFolkArtist
Instagram: @rebekah_lsmith

Photo by Tessa Christine Smith

Kelsey Anilee Smith

Kelsey Anilee Smith has loved all things old from a young age. Growing up with folks who collected remnants of the past and shared history, this was practically an inherited trait. Nevertheless, it was a passion of her own and led her to earning a bachelor of arts in history from Cleveland State University and a master of arts in museum studies from Indiana University—Purdue University Indianapolis.

Her work in museums and love of studying the past continually inspires her work. Beginning as a Fraktur artist in the Pennsylvania German style, she eventually dabbled with embroidery and fell in love with stitching.

Visit Kelsey online and follow on social media!
Website: kelseyanilee.com
Facebook: /kelseyanilee
Instagram: @kelseyanilee_designs

Also by Rebekah L. Smith:

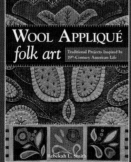

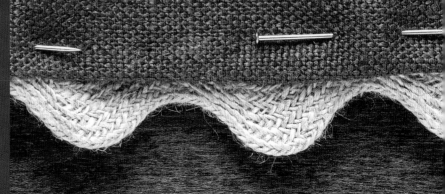

Want even more creative content?

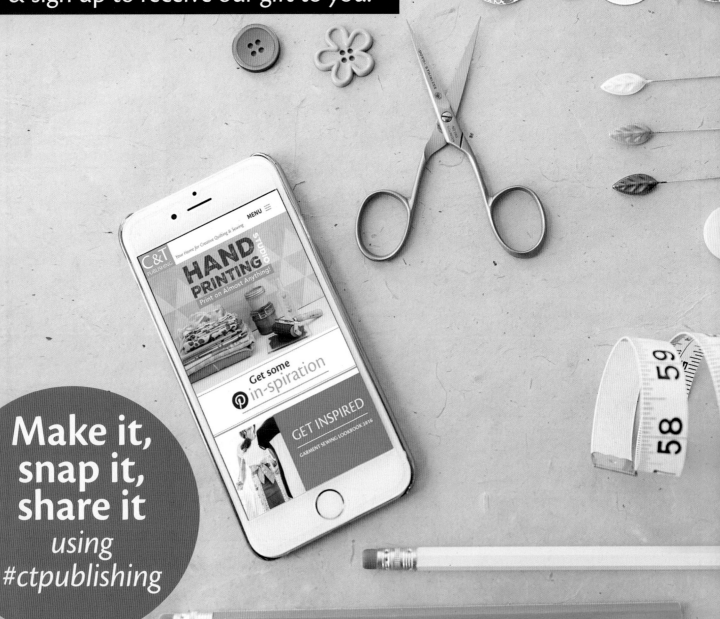

Make it, snap it, share it *using #ctpublishing*